# Left Letters

# LEFT LETTERS

The Culture Wars of
Mike Gold and
Joseph Freeman

James D. Bloom

Columbia University Press
New York

Columbia University Press
New York   Oxford
Copyright © 1992 Columbia University Press
All rights reserved

Library of Congress Cataloging-in-Publication Data

Bloom, James D.
   Left letters : the culture wars of Mike Gold and Joseph Freeman /
James D. Bloom.
      p.   cm.
   Includes bibliographical references (p.   ) and index.
   ISBN 0–231–07690–8
   1. Gold, Michael, 1894–1967—Criticism and interpretation.
   2. Freeman, Joseph, 1987–1965—Criticism and interpretation.
   3. American prose literature—20th century—History and criticism.
   4.Politics and literature—United States—History—20th century.
   5. Criticism—United States—History—20th century.   6. United
States—Intellectual life—20th century.   7. Communism and literature—
United States.   I. Title.
   PS3513.O29Z59   1992
818'.520809—dc20                                                      91–37291
                                                                          CIP

Casebound editions of Columbia University Press books are
Smyth-sewn and printed on permanent and durable acid-
free paper.

Printed in the United States of America

© 10 9 8 7 6 5 4 3 2 1

For Robin and Willem

*In Memory*

Bessie Bloom (1891–1979)
Joseph Bloom (1885–1955)
Anna Singer (1891–1975)
Oscar Singer (1888–1944)

Our capacity to take seriously views of the world which we do not accept as true is both the principal strength and weakness of our discipline.

—Burton Hatlen, "Why Is *The Education of Henry Adams* 'Literature' While *The Theory of the Leisure Class* Is Not?"

The arts, you know, they're Jews. They're left-wing. In other words, stay away.

—Richard Nixon, White House Tapes

# Contents

# Acknowledgments

As I was completing this book, I learned of the death of Michael Folsom (1938–1990). Everyone who has studied Mike Gold is indebted to Folsom, who struggled and even suffered to keep Gold's legacy alive.

My other debts are extensive.

Alan Wald and Morris Dickstein gave astute and thorough criticism, essential advice, and crucial encouragment.

Jennifer Crewe orchestrated the project and provided support when it was most essential, and Susan Pensak graciously reminded me of my oversights and helped me finish this project with renewed confidence.

Arthur Casciato and Avis Berman showed me where to find what I needed.

In answering my *New York Times Book Review* query, several correspondents provided leads I'm likely to have otherwise gone without. They included Tillie Pevzner, Tiba Willner, Elanor Quirt, Andre Ruellan, Morris Schappes, Malvine Cole, Rose Scheuer, Stanley Burnshaw, Herbert Kline, Robert Gorham Davis, John Halberstadt, Roseanne Singer. Michael Anderson at the *Times* helped put me in touch with these witnesses.

Tom Cartelli and Peter Edidin read and commented on my manuscript when it most needed frank, friendly criticism.

Muhlenberg librarians—especially Scherelene Schatz, Chris Fiedler, Marianne Bundra, Susan Silsbee—got me what I was looking for.

Librarians at Stanford's Hoover Institution, NYU's Fales Collection, the University of Pennsylvania, and the Smithsonian Institution's Archives of American Art generously allowed me access to their collections.

Essential logistical and clerical support came from Carol Proctor, Duiane Laubach and the Muhlenberg print shop, and the Muhlenberg mail-room crew.

Colleagues whose lively discussions of books, movies, critical theories, history, and politics kept my mind open and my curiosity alive as I worked on this book include Robin Beaty, Martha Smith, Mark Edmundson, David Rosenwasser, Jill Stephen, Anna Adams, Grant Scott, Mary Lawlor, Steve Schearier, Jim Schneider, members of Morris Dickstein's 1988 NEH Seminar, and participants in Maria Rose Logan's monthly humanities seminars at Muhlenberg.

Several students challenged me with their responses to *Jews Without Money* and *The Book of Daniel*. They kept me reconsidering what I thought I knew about these books.

My gratitude to Robin Beaty is beyond calculation.

# Left Letters

# Left Reading: An Introduction

Never has there been a a cause so bad that it has not
been defended by good men for good reasons.
                                        —John O'Leary

I got the bourgeois blues, baby, spread the news
around.                                  —Leadbelly

The names of Mike Gold (1893–1967) and Joseph Freeman (1897–1965) appear throughout the cultural histories and the literary annals
of the 1920s and particularly the 1930s as perhaps the most prominent literary Communists
of the era. Despite this ubiquity, their work as
writers and their influence as cultural politi-
cians, the ways in which they strove to make
themselves "agents of the Zeitgeist" (Rahv 4),
have gone nearly unexamined in the half century since they made their mark. In the following chapters, I examine what they accomplished
and what they set out to achieve. Freeman suc-
cinctly described their agenda as editors of the
*New Masses;* as contributing editors to the land-
mark 1935 anthology *Proletarian Literature in the
United States;* as authors of acclaimed autobiographical narratives—Gold's *Jews Without Money*
(1930) and Freeman's *An American Testament*
(1936)—and of numerous essays: to bring "rev-

olutionary literature and criticism . . . out in the open world of the living American" ("Ivory" 24). In a letter to John Dos Passos a year later, Edmund Wilson described the extent to which these "agitators'" efforts succeeded in making "their influence . . . felt" by raising "fundamental questions," despite their "failing to live up to their pretensions" (*Letters* 257).

Over the past generation, the academic study of literature and, to a lesser extent, various lay practices of it have become, as conservative and reactionary observers complain, increasingly leftist (Menand 19–20). As David Simpson observed a few years ago, "Suddenly it is fashionable . . . to be called a Marxist" (722). (For their methodological and epistemological precision, *materialist* and *agnostic* may describe the salutary aspects of this development more aptly than more familiar, tried but not so true adjectives I use warily throughout this book: the hagiographic *Marxist* or the obsolescent nineteenth-century French metonymy *leftist*.) Pursuing this kind of inquiry, many of us who teach literature now ask questions such as "Is there a class in this text?" (Berkhofer 600). Such broadly Marxist questions, which stress materialist heuristics rather than utopian doctrine, now pervade—albeit uneasily—academic literary study (Jay).

Writing in 1934, Joe Freeman recalled a time when he and "Mike Gold were the only literary critics asking such questions" ("Ivory" 22). V. F. Calverton assessed Gold's influence sixty years ago, while he was exerting it: "*Jews Without Money* was one of the most popular novels—or shall we call it autobiography? in 1930—[and Gold] is the second most important revolutionary writer in this country. . . . He has exerted, no doubt, greater influence over young revolutionary compatriots [than John Dos Passos]" (463). By the end of the thirties, even the more judicious and ambivalently Marxist critic Edmund Wilson acknowledged how much literary Communists, and especially Gold, changed American literary culture in the thirties (*Shores* 500, 539). Since the thirties, this movement has continued to exert a formative influence. Thus Lionel Trilling insisted that

in any view of the American cultural situation, the importance of the Thirties cannot be overestimated. It may be said to have created the American intellectual class as we now know it. The political style of the Thirties defined the style of the class—from that radicalism came the urgency, the sense of crisis, and the concern with personal salvation that mark the existence of American intellectuals. (*Last* 15–16)

Freeman's and Gold's contributions to this transformation have been sympathetically documented (Aaron, *Writers* 86–109, 178–81, 377–80), summarized (Gilbert, "Literature" 165; Klehr 70–75), noted (Said 160), and appreciated even by unsympathetic historians (Howe and Coser 277, 283). Nonetheless, their work has remained on the margins of literary history, even in histories of oppositional writing. Frank Kermode, for example, recently revealed this marginality by misnaming Mike Gold "Herbert Gold" while arguing that we need to value Communist writers of the thirties more than we have (*History* 36). Another symptom of this neglect is the omission of Gold and Freeman in David Bromwich's recent genealogy of "Literary Radicalism in America," a title that promises much more than it delivers, from the recent collection entitled *A Choice of Inheritance*. Whether Gold, Freeman, and the literary Communists connected with the *New Masses*, which achieved the "widest circulation of radical little magazines" in the thirties (Gilbert 165), were insufficiently literary or too indecorously radical for Bromwich remains an open question. Bromwich's legacy of "choice," "the Eliotic-Trotskyist" *Partisan Review* strain of literary radicalism that developed in the thirties, depends on his denying the occurrence of any significant activity by "literary radicals" between the death of Randolph Bourne and the second birth of the *Partisan Review* as a platform for anti-Stalinism and the promotion of European modernisms. Bromwich's genealogy represses the formative conflict that produced this retrospectively triumphant, ostensibly representative left elitism.

In striking contrast, Robert Warshow, who came of age in the thirties, remembered—indignantly—how Communists set the American cultural agenda of the period. Writers like Gold and Freeman helped shape this agenda through the *New Masses* and other periodicals, through Alexander Trachtenberg's International Publishers, through writers' congresses, and, early in the decade, through a nationwide network of John Reed Clubs. In Warshow's account, "The Legacy of the Thirties," "Virtually all intellectual vitality was derived . . . from the Communist party" (33). Even the Communists' opponents—like Bromwich's Eliotic-Trotskyists—found that the Communist agenda "ultimately determined what you were to think about and in what terms."

Omissions such as Bromwich's may be, in part, a legitimate reaction to the tragic mistake Gold and Freeman made—and Gold crudely, loudly, ever more marginally repeated and perpetuated—in not repudiating Stalinism as soon as the atrocities it rested on became known. But beyond the tragic self-destruction of American Communism such omissions also seemed to be a cumulative product of subsequent developments: McCarthyism in the fifties and the formalist antihistoricist New Criticism it fostered (Franklin 113); the "heedless confidence" in the sixties of the so-called New Left "that they were destined to succeed where their elders had failed" (Iserman 216, 215); and, more recently, a mandarin academic "Marxism" whose "covertly idealist" adherents disdain as vulgar or philistine attention to the immediate civic consequences and material contradictions of their intellectual practice (Simpson 722–25). Thus, according to Ihab Hassan, "Marxism returns as a 'theory' to our academies, a theory without any credible continuity with praxis in the West" (134).

This failure of academic Marxism, its lack of practical political leverage, and its surrender of the rhetorical authority of populism to bigots and plutocrats doesn't jibe with its persistence as "theory." This persistence reflects a thwarted will to recover the rhetorical authority and the moral legitimacy traditionally associated with democratic egalitarianism in this country, which overrides purely theoretical demands of rigor and consistency. Here the literary Marxisms of today and those of Gold and Freeman meet, though the earlier generation was less defensive about its jeremiadic fervor and hortatory moralizing. An example of this family resemblance and generational divergence that might highlight the cautionary and emulative lessons of this study is a recent manifesto essay by Michael Ryan.

Ryan set out to refute the essay by Ihab Hassan cited above and began by lifting his title verbatim from Gold's 1932 autobiographical confession "Why I Am a Communist" (*Anthology* 209–14). Ryan's argument rests on his boasts of being a victim—of "reactionaries . . . liberals . . . Stalinist commissars" who "trash . . . dump on . . . come after" the beleaguered author. He concludes by congratulating himself for "shocking" his derisively implied reader. By contrast, Gold's precursor essay, a legacy Ryan never acknowledges, made its case for Communism without Ryan's whimpering self-aggrandizement. Gold began self-effacingly by acknowledging his debt to earlier Communists and even to nineteenth-century Romantics (210–11). Unlike Ryan, Gold also admitted "mistakes" (213) and conceded the crudity of his position (214). Despite Gold's falsifying of historical facts (in asserting that the Communists made the Russian Revolution), his position rests not on sanctimonious generalization but on autobiography, the sort of acccessibly "vulgar" detail that Ryan, in keeping with strictures of academic "rigor," avoids.

Ryan's petulant Marxism and Bromwich's aloof mandarinism illustrate the range of elisions, strictures, and revisionist deformations informing recent literary history. One result, which Antonio Gramsci foresaw over half a century ago, is that "Marxism itself has become a 'prejudice' and 'superstition' " (87). Underlying the genealogical explorations that follow is the hope that an attentive exhumation of America's earliest literary Marxists will help erode this superstition.

As part of this recovery, Cold War views of these writers' works, especially Gold's fiction, as crude, sentimental
agitprop, need to be reconsidered and perhaps revised.
Now that Communism no longer has much status as a persuasive, revolutionary alternative to the long-established,
uneasily evolving political and economic organization of
life in the industrial West—a compelling new reason to
hope that Stalinism will become a troubling, fascinating
historical problem, no longer a demonizing name for mass
murder or a reproach to the integrity of nonviolent lef-
tisms—readers can study writings by Communists without having to fear that such attention constitutes an endorsement of the gulag and the Hitler-Stalin treaty, which
Gold stood by and Freeman dissociated himself from
slowly and traumatically. Perhaps we can now reexamine
these writers, free of the shackles Vivian Gornick sought
to break open over a decade ago:

For thirty years now people have been writing about the Communists with an oppressive distance between themselves and
their subject, a distance that often masquerades as objectivity but
in fact conveys only an emotional and intellectual atmosphere of
"otherness"—as though something not quite recognizable,
something vaguely nonhuman was being described. . . . This is
the language of men who have assumed an intellectual opposition to the human falsifications inherent in the Communist passion, and in the process are themselves committing human falsifications. Denouncing a monolithic political reality that is
summed up in one armor-plated word . . . "Stalinism" . . . , they
deny the teeming, contradictory life behind the word. (18–19)

Robert Frost once complained about the tendency to
confuse voting and thinking. The substitution of the former for the latter was especially pronounced during the
thirties and persists in much of the retrospect on this period by those who participated in the cultural life of the
decade. Free now to think about the Communists of the
period without feeling compelled to "vote," readers can
discover how works like *Jews Without Money* and *An American Testament* manifest the complexity and pay the self-
conscious attention to their words that, broadly speaking,

makes a text "literary"; how, more particularly, those works show the density, the generic ambiguity, and the understanding of their own production and their own status as mediated and mediating cultural products that make the most memorable writing of the past century and a half "modernist" (Poirier 131). As early as 1934, Trilling directed readers to the artistry in some proletarian writing and suggested that we can treat this artistry as integral to these works' overt advocacy without losing sight of their partisan agendas (*Speaking* 86–87). Trilling's program informs the readings that follow—of *Jews Without Money,* one of the lasting narratives that the proletarian movement produced; and of Freeman's three sustained narratives, *An American Testament* and two subsequent novels. Whether labeled novel or autobiography, each of these narratives evokes transforming experiences that make an example, a fiction, and perhaps a fable of the writer's life.

Thomas Bender recently—and perhaps too selectively—honored the "literariness" of such writing by singling out Gold as the "most consistent and most gifted of of literary Communists" (246). In an account of her coming-of-age as a New York intellectual in the thirties, Lucy Dawidowicz remembers him as "the most gifted writer the Communists ever completely captured" (18). Lewis Mumford, who lamented Gold's wasted talent (a mild reaction to Gold's vituperative attacks on Mumford in 1940 as a fascist "renegade"), could still look back generously on *Jews Without Money* as "a significant but minor monument" (*Sketches* 113; cf. 135).

One of many talented and influential literary Communists, Gold seems the most widely remembered. Less monumental, less flamboyant, less "consistent" than Gold, Joseph Freeman made less of a mark. His work may therefore need an even more extensive recovery. Theodore Draper, another retrospective antagonist of thirties Communism, designated Freeman's *American Testament* "one of the few Communist documents worth preserving" (129). Such judgments inform this project.

This work of recovery has been unevenly under way for

the past generation. The most influential efforts are Daniel Aaron's substantially testimonial *Writers on the Left* and Marcus Klein's *Foreigners,* which demonstrates the enlivening and metamorphosing impact of left insurgence, immigrant assimilation, and class antagonism on American writing in the thirties. Fortunately, chronic obstacles to this recovery, in force throughout the two decades between Aaron's book and Klein's, seem to be diminishing, with Cary Nelson's *Repression and Recovery* the notable contribution of the past decade.

A significant new condition is the academic literati's commitment to revising and expanding canons (the grouping of writers and works that professors want students to know about). The new Heath anthology of American literature, for example, has become the first comprehensive classroom anthology to include Mike Gold. Globally, the worldwide discrediting of Communism as theoretical template for social and political relationships and the consequent erosion of U.S.-Soviet enmity has removed another obstacle to treating Gold and Freeman as writers rather than as symptoms.

Beyond recovering Gold's and Freeman's work, I have set out to demonstrate their engagement with issues that now preoccupy literary theorists: to show how their writing characteristically contests the representation of social experience—mostly the work of "superficial liars" according to Gold (J 71)—and criticizes established texts. Texts of choice include writing of the official Anglo-American literary canon from Shakespeare through Hemingway, which both writers selectively honored and resisted, and works of popular culture, especially from the press and the movies. Since the motive of such textual contestation was frankly to "change the world" (the allusively Marxist title of Gold's regular column in the *Daily Worker*), I've borrowed the German compound Kulturkampf—literally "culture-struggle"—to name the sort of effort that both writers devoted themselves to. Associated with Bismarck's consolidation and modernization of Germany in the 1870s, the term was actually introduced by a left liberal Bundesrat deputy to describe "the great struggle for civilization in the interest of humanity" (Craig 74). Hence the ironic resonance of Kulturkampf when applied to Gold and Freeman recalls their will to progressive democratic change and to the transformation of a citizenry's consciousness through the adaptive appropriation of a culture's myths and icons (Klein, *Foreigners* 89–90). The German noun recalls, too, the fatal embrace such hopes engendered: an embrace of Stalin who exploited progressive hopes far more monstrously than Bismarck before him.

The literary Communists of the thirties repeatedly presented themselves as Kulturkampf warriors, "participating in a battle . . . for civilization" according to Granville Hicks (Leitch, *American* 12). Thus Freeman declared in 1930 that "American literature is going through a violent war" ("Social Trends"). Five years later, he devoted much of his introduction to *Proletarian Literature in the United States* to establishing the connection between "art" and "class struggle" (12, 18). Even after leaving the Communist party, Freeman retrospectively endorsed the literary leftism of the thirties as a "popular movement for the preservation of nineteenth-century democratic ideals against the onslaught of fascism" ("Biographical" 902). Gold also used expressly martial imagery and so linked literary avant-gardism with revolutionary Communist aspirations; thus he praised Jack Conroy's novel *The Disinherited* as an "advance-guard skirmish in a great battle" (*CW* 216). Regardless of which side won or which side was right, the perennially valuable insight in such claims lies in the scruple against presuming Olympian distance from culture: "The Communists not only deny that art is something apart from the social structure; they further deny that artists are 'above the battle'" (Freeman, *Voices* 17). Though we needn't endorse this party-line view of "art as a weapon," we can't easily dismiss the thirties-inspired view of literature, especially of criticism, as inevitably embattled.

As Trilling lamented at the end of the thirties, war had become the prevailing metaphor among literati for how culture works (*Speaking* 118). Some sixty years later, hardly anyone denies that such "battles" persist. Thus the president of the Modern Language Association recently urged her constituents to attend to "contemporary wars" over "the nature of cultural authority" (Stimpson 2). To her right, the proudly reactionary radio commentator Rush Limbaugh recently ratified this understanding of how culture works, as "'culture war . . . between upholding decent values—conservatives—and the commie-lib hordes trying to devalue human life" (Grossberger 95).

This is the climate for which, I hope to demonstrate, the examples of Mike Gold and Joseph Freeman have a decided relevance. Thus my dependence throughout *Left Letters* on literary theorist-politicians now influential in the academy—Lentricchia, Kermode, Said, Jameson, Arac,—constitutes a bid to bring Gold's and Freeman's work to bear on ongoing conversations among my colleagues: about the possibility of coordinating rhetorical profession and political practice; about the dialectics of literary representation and historical change; about the role of cultural contestation in authorial careers; and about the very criteria of literariness.

Too often nonacademic readers, who have a stake in the culture wars that apparently rage around them, are served up such culture struggle as the degenerate sport of perverse academics—George Will interviewing Allan Bloom or *Newsweek* sidebars on Stanley Fish. Such packaging obscures more pervasive, usually narrative forms that culture war takes. Since lay readers may know American literary Communism (if they know it at all) through Gold's *Jews Without Money* (the only work of Gold or Freeman still in-print), my readings link Gold's writing to more familiar contemporary works, novels that at once wage and probe culture war. For example, E. L. Doctorow's *The Book of Daniel* revises the left legacy Gold and Freeman helped construct and Philip Roth's *Goodbye Columbus* recasts the immigrant-assimilation lore that Gold and Freeman helped naturalize. My readings also relate their work to the writing of their contemporaries—Henry Roth's *Call It*

*Sleep* and Jack Conroy's *The Disinherited*—and to some immediate, widely influential precursor texts—Abraham Cahan's *The Rise of David Levinsky* and *The Education of Henry Adams.*

Freeman's and Gold's work as culture warriors included critical fascination with the familiar Hollywood and media-made celebrity culture of their time—the familiar milieux of Walter Winchell and Shirley Temple—at a time when influential academics and critics scorned serious attention to current popular entertainment. Gold's and Freeman's contribution to legitimating critical analytic attention to the production and consumption of mass culture, especially of the movies, prefigures the current, rising academic interest in popular culture.

At the same time that Gold and Freeman took an interest in the elite and demotic cultures of their time, they were obliged to promote the often procrustean and unpredictably varying positions of the Communist party. Inevitably this resulted in much contradiction and egregious lapses of rigor and even honesty. Since similar difficulties pervade literary writing and cultural politics today, we may have a great deal to learn from Gold and Freeman, who were caught up in these contradictions and lapses half a century ago. What follows is an effort to evoke these contradictions and to demonstrate how Freeman's and Gold's autobiographical writing enacts and wages the Kulturkampf that their manifestos, reviews, and theoretical essays advocate and promote. These evocations and demonstrations rest on selective biographical documentation, on an analysis of representative texts, and on an account of the cultural materials Gold and Freeman worked with. My applications of biography and close reading are means to an end: the integration of Freeman and Gold into the literary history many of us are committed to remaking. I look forward to their achievements and failures receiving increased and increasingly diverse attention, including full-dress biographies and readings that will challenge and complement my own.

My first chapter establishes the "literariness" of Gold's

and perhaps the thirties proletarian movement's best-known fiction, *Jews Without Money,* against the backdrop of the brief revival of interest in Gold and his legacy around 1970. This chapter focuses on perhaps the most lasting manifestation of this revival, E. L. Doctorow's intertextual appropriation of *Jews Without Money* in *The Book of Daniel.* The next chapter casts Gold as a Communist Caliban in order to demonstrate how *Jews Without Money* and Gold's complementary criticism and polemics wage Kultur-kampf—on behalf of "proletarian realism" and against the class- and ethnic-based monopolies that governed Anglo-American literary culture. In evoking his revisionist assaults and subversions, I examine Gold's critique and appropriation of other writers—Shakespeare, Blake, Emerson, Wilder, MacLeish—and his even more encompassing mastery of a wide array of literary and extraliterary utterance and representation. Chapter 3 links Gold and his fellow culture warrior Freeman and then focuses on Freeman's career, showing a markedly different, more theoretical and more traditionally "literary" brand of literary Communism. Here I look closely at Freeman's three major books: a long autobiographical account of his conversion to Communism and two novels, *Never Call Retreat* and *The Long Pursuit,* written after Freeman left the party. In accordance with current theoretical views, I don't treat the autobiography, *An American Testament,* merely as a documentary record. Rather, I've bracketed it with the two novels as works in an ongoing *apologia pro sua vita* and failed mythography. The final chapter limns some of the broader problems that Gold and Freeman grappled with as early literary Marxists: the modernisms whose influence Gold and Freeman couldn't avoid and the more encompassing impositions of modernity, including assembly-line "Fordism," skyscrapers, and Hollywood, that their politics obliged them to account for.

# 1  A Searching Seizure

When he was growing up, the word *socialist* had religious overtones. It was like *Zealot* and *Masada*. There was something Jewish about it. No matter how wrongheaded a socialist might be, no matter how cruel and vindictive, he possessed somewhere in his soul a spark of the light of God, of Yahweh.

—Tom Wolfe, *The Bonfire of the Vanities*

a larger need to which Marxism spoke and which the Communist Party embodied: the need within the human spirit to say no to the judgment of man upon man that is the politicalness of life. Nothing in the twentieth century has spoken as compellingly—with such power and moral imagination—as has Communism; nothing in modern times has so joined the need with the real and the ideal to produce a universe of internal experience as has Communism.

—Vivian Gornick, *The Romance of American Communism*

"Tell Mike Gold that Ernest Hemingway says he should go fuck himself" (Pyros 151). That this philippic came in the 1940s when Hemingway was the brightest star in the firmament of American novelists and Mike Gold's single lasting work of fiction was a decade behind him seems especially puzzling. Other writers, also immeasurably more famous and influential than Mike Gold, have, over the years, reacted with similar vehemence to Gold and his work. Thomas Wolfe, for example, responded to the suggestion that he might learn something from Gold with a belligerently rhetorical question: "Why in hell doesn't Mike Gold write like me?" (Donald 455). Even presumably scholarly accounts of his work deteriorate into slander—vehement denials of Gold's achievement as a writer and his invigorating effect on the literary culture of the 1930s (Howe and Coser 277; Hofstadter 293; Fiedler, *Jew* 31; Lasch, *Agony* 54). What is so threatening about Gold, his work, and what he represents? Even as recently as 1990, twenty-three years after Gold died in obscurity, Hilton Kramer's *New Criterion* singled out Gold as "a bleak exemplar of literary Stalinism" (Tanenhaus 16).

Gold's frank, dogged adherence to Soviet Communism enraged not only Lost Generation novelists like Wolfe and Hemingway whose lofty calling as artists has, in most accounts, earned them places beyond their partisan position-taking. Gold's obstinate misguided allegiance during the years after most prominent literary Communists and fellow travelers broke with the Communist party also threatened the generation of intellectuals and academics who believed themselves to be working after "the end of ideology." Hence the easy acceptance of intemperate attacks on Gold by such Olympian liberal authorities as Richard Hofstadter and Irving Howe. Thanks to them, "hack" or "hatchetman" are usually the first words uttered by most readers who react at all on hearing the name Mike Gold. This reductive view of Gold as a bully and a vulgarian, which Gold himself helped foster, has unfortunately effaced his achievement as a writer in the late 1920s and the early 1930s.

Since the 1970s, though, the politics that govern literary practice and study have again been sanctioning ideological inquiry and even advocacy, inviting thoughtful readers to acknowledge the ideological ground that our lives and work rests on. Moreover, a new generation of left-minded intellectuals has come of age and achieved some prominence unburdened by guilty or self-congratulatory revulsion from Stalinism, a recoil that targeted Gold and inflated his undeniable offenses against conscience and reason. Unlike Gold's midcentury critics, readers now can approach Gold with greater openness than preceding generations. As Jonathan Arac points out, "Trilling's generation. . . . eradicated from American culture the dangers of Stalinism" and left their successors "free to explore new possibilities on the left" (314). One of the first American works of fiction to make this turn and to pursue this New Left agenda was E. L. Doctorow's 1971 novel *The Book of Daniel*, which coincided with efforts by Mike Folsom and Jack Salzman to rehabilitate Mike Gold. The publication of Doctorow's novel came between the paperback reissue of Gold's one, very popular 1930 novel-autobiography, *Jews Without Money*, in 1966, and Michael Folsom's anthology of Gold's criticism in 1972. Though more obliquely than these efforts, *The Book of Daniel* also contributes to this recovery of Gold's legacy and to the larger legacies that Doctorow's novels repeatedly honor: the writing of American agitators dating back to Thomas Paine; the sort of socially engaged fiction that prevailed in American literature during the Depression and the Progressive period, which Doctorow comically and chillingly evoked in *Ragtime*; the destructive ironies of individualism—of becoming a self-made man—limned repeatedly by Dreiser and by Doctorow in *Loon Lake* and *Billy Bathgate*.

Nowhere is Doctorow's critical radicalism more pronounced than in *The Book of Daniel*. Doctorow loosely based this novel on the careers of Ethel and Julius Rosenberg as members of the Communist party accused of and executed for spying for the Soviet Union. Early in the novel, as Doctorow's eponymous narrator describes his Rosenberg-like parents' arrest, he recalls and catalogues their confiscated belongings, all "valuable things" to him.

This is what they took: my crystal radio and my radio for listening. A stack of selected newspapers. My father's International Workers' Order insurance policy for five thousand dollars. A toolbox. A year's issues of *Masses* and *Mainstream*. And the fol-

lowing books: JEWS WITHOUT MONEY by Mike Gold, THE
IRON HEEL by Jack London, STATE AND REVOLUTION by V.
Lenin, GENE DEBS, THE STORY OF A FIGHTING AMERICAN
by Herbert Marais and William Cahn, THE PRICE OF FREE
WORLD VICTORY by Henry A. Wallace, THE GREAT CON-
SPIRACY by Michael Sayers and Albert E. Kahn, WHO OWNS
AMERICA by James S. Allen. (140)

The first book that Daniel names, *Jews Without Money,* has
remained among the most durable products in an ephemeral genre, proletarian fiction, programmatically conceived
and widely attempted during the 1930s (Pyros 24–27). If a
noncanonic program such as proletarian fiction can be said
to have produced any classics, then Gold's single novel is
its classic, not just a classic of proletarian fiction but of
American protest writing (Dickstein, "Hallucinating" 163).
Such was the book's resonance when first published that
Sinclair Lewis, in his Nobel Prize acceptance speech,
paired Gold with Faulkner in prophesying a glorious future for American literature. Thus Doctorow's reference to
*Jews Without Money* and the priority Doctorow assigns it
establish it as an authoritative precursor text in a long
discredited genre. Doctorow's identification of "the relationship between radical movements of one generation
and another" (LeClair and McCaffrey 104) as a central concern in his novel suggests a genealogical explanation for
Gold's presence and primacy here: an assumption that the
radical Jewish novel derives from Gold whose criticism in
the twenties and thirties repeatedly proposed a revolutionary literary agenda and whose narratives and politics
drew repeatedly on his Lower East Side ghetto coming-of-
age. As a representative story of a son ·of immigrants
growing up in poverty and growing increasingly angry
about the causes and consequences of that poverty, *Jews
Without Money* also calls to mind the background of the
Isaacsons, the narrator's parents, in *The Book of Daniel.*
They too were, like Gold and his autobiographical narrator, the children of ghetto-bound immigrants—"Jews
without money" for whom Communism promised redemption. This broad correspondence begins to account

for the place of Gold's book on Daniel's list in Doctorow's novel.

Daniel's detailed catalogue consists almost entirely of printed texts. Todd Gitlin has glibly dismissed such "garage sale lists" as a symptom of postmodernist indifference, a token of the prevailing will to resist criticism and commitment that Gitlin has ascribed to *The Book of Daniel* ("Hip-Deep"). Doctorow's narrative context here, however, very pointedly positions this text as a synecdochic act of criticism and commitment. Most obviously, the texts here form a canon—an inchoate countercanon—of progressive/revolutionary representations. The sequential proximity of the first two works, Gold's novel and Jack London's apocalyptic revolutionary prophecy, *The Iron Heel,* recalls Gold's own anxiety to claim a dissident literary inheritance (Gold, *Anthology* 189; Gilbert, *Writers* 14). Moreover, these texts and the homemade radio set that Daniel also recalls are all media of cultural transmission and self-representation. These media stand out as the only wholes, the only objects with any integrity, that survive his parents' arrest, the shattering sense of violation, and the chilling isolation that follows. The descriptions of the Isaacson apartment and of Daniel himself that frame this list evoke this disruption and destruction, in contrast to the clarity and orderlines of Daniel's reassuring, ideologically consonant list of texts:

Daniel ran back to his room. His own blue tin filled with pennies of peculiar existence had been opened and the pennies scattered on the floor. Downstairs the place was a shambles. Broken dishes in the kitchen. The newspapers from under the stairs strewn about. . . . A terrible draft swept through the house now, the front door having been propped open. . . . Daniel stood in the living room. He was still in his pajamas. The cold of the morning had driven itself into his chest. It filled his chest and throat. It pressed the backs of his eyes. He was frightened by the way he felt. The cold hung like ice from his heart. His little balls were encased in ice. (139–140)

By associating broken kitchenware, an emblem of shattered domestic security, and the loss of Daniel's paltry child's capital with torn newspapers, Doctorow reinforces the importance of texts to Daniel and the precarious, ephemeral status of representation in the culture at large. This concern pervades the novel as a whole, which announces its own textuality in its title with the word *book*. "This is a significant stricture. The man who chose the . . . title, who chose everything carefully in his novel, presumably had two reasons for it. First, the Old Testament resonance, the suggestion of the prophetic mission and of the Jewishness specific to the material. Second, the essence of the novel. The essence is the writing of a book within the novel. Daniel's attempt to write that book is the dynamic of what goes on in Doctorow's book" (Kauffmann). In an otherwise difficult narrative, one characteristic of Doctorow's novel stands out: this is a book about books, about how we make them, about how they make us, and mostly about how we use them.

Doctorow establishes this feature repeatedly, with recurring textual references and allusions—to Dickens (117), to James (256), to Salinger (198), to Poe (218), to Eisenstein (193). As much recent criticism has demonstrated, such allusiveness enables a writer simultaneously to claim, canonize, and criticize his or her cultural legacy (Nadel 56–62). Such an effort seems to underlie Daniel's countercanonical list making, in which Daniel assigns *Jews Without Money* pride of place. The list acknowledges indebtedness while inviting reassessment of how we understand and value the work and the writer recalled. This effort corresponds to what Edward Said, distinguishing "filiation" and "affiliation," describes as "the transition from a failed idea or possibility of filiation to a kind of compensatory order . . . a party, an institution . . . culture . . . beliefs . . . a new relationship . . . a new system" (19). This transition figures prominently in both Gold's and Doctorow's first-person fiction: in each narratively disjointed *Bildungsroman* compensatory intellectual commitments and ideological affiliation displace "natural" parental affiliations. In each book the narrator's loss of his parents—to imprisonment and execution or to chronic depression and socioeconomic marginality—parallels the narrator's passage from nature to culture (cf. Said 20). Thus Doctorow's reference here to Gold's work signals a decisive affiliative move.

The abundance and diversity of Doctorow's references and allusions reflect, moreover, the radical rhetorical motives that intertextuality often produces, the subversion of a presumably familiar context. "Intertextuality, a text's dependence on and infiltration by prior codes, concepts, conventions, unconscious practices, and texts, appears here as . . . a strategic instrument. . . . Intertextuality subverts context. . . . It exposes all contextualizations as limited and limiting, arbitrary and confining, self-serving and authoritarian, theological and political. . . . Intertextuality offers a liberating determinism" (Leitch, *Criticism* 161–62).

Gold's book figures as an especially resonant "intertext" in *The Book of Daniel*. This resonance rests on Doctorow's affiliative dependence on and critical readings and misreadings of thirties Communism, the subculture widely disparaged until recently as "the Old Left" (18, 66, 235–39; Olster 145–46), an intellectually shoddy product of "vulgar Marxism."

Early in *The Book of Daniel* Daniel recollects his father's lecture on the "*real* purpose" of major league baseball: "The economic class of baseball fans. Why they needed baseball. What would happen to the game if people had enough money, enough freedom" (43). Daniel's reconstruction of his Communist father's effort—one of many—"to exorcize the bad influences" (42) mimics one of Gold's regular "Change the World" columns in the *Daily Worker*. "Like everything else in this country, baseball is not run for the fans, but for the pockets of the stockholders. Communists are often ridiculed for insistence that everything in the present capitalist system is a "racket.' . . . Workers love baseball. But baseball, in its own way, is used as an 'opium of the people' " (CW 98–100).

Entitled "Baseball Is a Racket," this column rehearsed the same sort of arguments that Daniel's father made. Daniel reinforces this view of his father as forming his politics, constructing these lectures through his partisan reading, by noting the abundance of *Daily Workers* and the *New Masses* in their house in the same passage in which Daniel cites *Jews Without Money* (139). Gold did as much as any left man-of-letters to produce and disseminate the conventional wisdom of the Old Left, the appealingly simple explanations now belittled as "vulgar Marxism" that Daniel's father shared with his son.

The modifier in the phrase *Old Left,* however, may misname the affiliative relationship between thirties Communism and Daniel's sixties protest culture, and may even reflect an effort on the part of the successor generation to diminish the sacrifice and repress the example of the precursors. "Russian tit-suckers" who "wore ties" and "held down jobs" runs the indictment of thirties Communists like Daniel's parents from Artie Sternlicht, a charismatic New Left leader who confronts the grown-up Daniel (185). Nevertheless, Daniel's own experience of sixties leftist martyrdom, arrest at a 1967 antiwar march, leads him to conclude that "it is a lot easier to be a revolutionary nowadays than it used to be" (314). Despite the self-congratulatory thrust of distinguishing old and new lefts, there was little intellectually primitive or "vulgar" and nothing originary—nothing "old"—about the so-called Old Left.

Mike Gold is a case in point. Writing for the *Liberator* and the *New Masses* during the 1920s and 1930s, Gold invoked precursors from Shelley to London, from Whitman to Randolph Bourne. "Gold belonged to the third generation of revolutionary American writers and recapitulated an old experience," according to his comrade and collaborator Joseph Freeman (*AT* 643). By beginning his revolutionary genealogy in his and Gold's own lifetime with London and Sinclair, Freeman selectively "forgets" the older and less programmatically "revolutionary" writers, particularly Twain and Dreiser, who shaped Gold (*Anthology* 306–7; *Reader* 182, 161; Turek 68, 77). Gold exhibited the same anxiety of influence implicit in our phrase *New Left,* selective attention and resistance to precursors that Freeman's promotion of Gold reinforced. He articulated his own proto-New Left cultural politics through the intertextual subversion and revisionist appropriation (*Anthology* 130, 138, 186–89; Gitlin, *Sixties* 5–6).

Gold's practice of this subtle sophisticated cultural politics belies the surviving image of him as a primitive sentimentalist, merely a Communist party mouthpiece. The very title of Gold's novel demonstrates his mastery of intertextual subversion and revisionist antagonism, his appreciation of their place in the culture wars that inform much celebrated modern literature. Consider Gold's explicit comments on this title in his introduction to a 1935 edition of *Jews Without Money*. Gold explained his title here as a defiant retort to the bigoted cliché it at once echoes and inverts, a counterrepresentation according to Gold:

A German friend told me . . . about her arrest by the Nazis . . . a week or so after Hitler had taken power. . . . She was translating a chapter from my book, "Jews Without Money," when armed Nazis broke in. The officer picked up some sheets of her manuscript, and read, "Jews Without Money." "Ho, ho!" he roared. "So there are Jews without money!" And all the Brown Shirts roared with him at the marvelous joke. How could there be Jews without money when, as every good Nazi knew . . . Jews were all international bankers?

Commenting on his anecdote, Gold added in editorial counterpoint an obvious economic fact of life: "The great mass of Jews today are not millionaire bankers, but paupers and workers." This counterpointing exemplifies Gold's ironic intertextuality, which here contests allusively influential texts like *Mein Kampf* and *The Protocols of the Elders of Zion* just as the countercliché that Gold's title announces discolors the genocidal cliché about "rich Jews" and "Jewish bankers" that Nazism rests on.

Most striking, though, to readers conditioned by misrepresentations of Gold as a crude anti-intellectual hack is his playful feel for the spoken word and his savoring of it throughout *Jews Without Money*, in which the marveling narrator evokes his boyhood beguilement by the gossiping, storytelling, and kitchen table declaiming of the voluble adults who surround him. As a result Gold's narrative displays the aural "density" that Richard Poirier associates with the most resonant products of literary modernism: "Density . . . strikes the ear rather than the eye . . . you hear [it] happening to voices as they modify words and phrases which, at another point, seemed quite clear and casual . . . gives evidence of human involvement in the shaping of language, and it prevents language from imposing itself upon us" (131).

Such resistant density is particularly evident in chapter 14 of *Jews Without Money*, "Buffalo Bill and the Messiah." Here the grown-up narrator opposes two of the most imposing discourses that he inhabited as a boy: the superstitious, obscurantist, "fanatic" and "neurotic," old-world Judaism of his parents (Jews 181) and the gentile popular culture that first attracts and finally repels the narrator. Temporarily the narrator can reconcile these cultural poles insofar as each, working like proverbially Marxist opiates, promises Messianic deliverance. Thus Gold's narrator recalls:

I believed the Messiah was coming, too. It was the one point in the Jewish religion I could understand clearly. We had no Santa Claus, but we had the Messiah. (184)

The thing pressed on my mind. I asked Reb Samuel. . . . He said the Messiah might not come for many years. He would ride a white horse and put to shame every enemy of the Jews. Would he look like Buffalo Bill? I asked. . . . I needed a Messiah who would look like Buffalo Bill. (190)

The defeat by "America" of messianic longing announced at the beginning of the very next chapter (191) confirms Gold's adult narrator's orthodox Marxist view of religious obscurantism. It marks the point where "the religious certainties of the *shtetl* give way to the radical certainties of the 1930s" and so helps prepare readers for the narrator's conversion at the end of *Jews* to an alternative messianic creed, Communism (Woolf 206)—from old-world "Jewish" deferral and deference to utopian action and assertiveness.

Doctorow's novel allows no such resolution. It is, as Stacey Olster argues, nonapocalyptic, countermillenarian, ideology refracting (2–4, 9). Consequently, Doctorow's narrative precludes the sort of coming-of-age that *Jews Without Money* so decisively enacts. In doing so, Doctorow maintains a dialogic density and a corresponding ideological openness, which Gold's ending shuts down. In relation to Gold's ghetto picaresque, the density of *Daniel* stands out in a section entitled "Alone in the Cold War with Franny and Zooey" (198–220), which is ostensibly an account of Daniel and his sister Susan's escape from the city shelter housing them during their parents imprisonment. Throughout this account, however, Daniel repeatedly interrupts himself to sound out and even savor words and names like "treason" and its Constitutional definition (205–6). Finally Daniel deliberately deranges Patrick Henry's defiant, exhilarating patriotic boast on behalf of treason, "if the this be treason make the most of it." Here Doctorow has Daniel reduce another one of his fragile, ultimately insupportable insights into his culture to gibberish: "If this be the reason make a mulch of it. . . . If this brie is in season drink some milk with it. . . . If this bitch is teasing make her post on it. . . . If this boy is breathing make a ghost of him" (206).

Though less developed, similar efforts to unravel accepted discourse—to reduce it to its component sound and fury—also mark Gold's novel. This construed dissonance enhances the narrator's programmatic sketch of his own mean streets, his effort to distill out of the surrounding dissonance a persuasive, politically correct discourse. For Doctorow, by contrast, such reduction-to-dissonance seems integral to his very different Kulturkampf, his sustained critique of all discourse as hindrance (Hutcheon 185). Hence the first intelligible sound in Gold's narrative, after a quick visual evocation of the narrator's Chrystie Street tenement, is the voice of parrot, cursing (13). Presumably, cursing is the most familiar kind of speech this parrot hears in Gold's ghetto, the very existence of which stands, according to Gold's narrator, as "a curse on Columbus! A curse on America, the thief!" (112). Cursing or "forbidden words" (158) form, as the narrator later learns from his mother, the most powerful language of defiance available to the powerless (see chapter 2).

Reflecting a similar understanding of cursing, the first directly quoted words in *Daniel* include a curse from the most decidedly powerless character in Doctorow's novel. In a "forbidden word" pronouncement that echoes throughout the novel, Daniel's sister Susan, straitjacketed and incarcerated, curses and leaves Daniel uncharacteristically speechless: "They're still fucking us" (10). In the next adult encounter between Daniel and Susan, she curses him as a "piece of shit" whose very life is an affront to their martyred parents (101). Susan's outburst elicits from Daniel an arid lecture to his readers on "the curse" as a "literary form." Undercutting the academic aridity of his appreciation, Daniel recalls that he learned about cursing from his immigrant grandmother: "rushing off, she would turn and shake her fist at the house and curse it in Yiddish, calling down cholera and Cossacks" (83). Daniel even recalls how "Grandma would curse him out, too." Characteristically playing the disinterested critic, he recalls how "it would become a very rhetorically involved curse."

Daniel provoked Susan's curses by ridiculing her politics: "She's a Revolutionary! She's got all the answers. She's been to the barricades" (101). Susan reacts to Daniel's taunt by invoking the revolutionary example of their parents and by continuing to curse: whether or not Susan's politics is mere posturing—impotent parody or parroting of their parents—as Daniel here charges, he has already admitted that politics for him involves images far more than it involves beliefs. "Images are what things mean" (88). Hence his third-person description of himself at the beginning of his book as *looking like* a "nineteen-thirties cafeteria commie" establishes the foremost "meaning" of Daniel (4). This genealogically specific self-image also helps account for the priority assigned Gold in Daniel's inventory. Of all the narratives, images, and discourses Daniel picks up and drops in *Daniel* the legacy of American Communism in the thirties, narratively, comes first.

This positioning reflects how much Doctorow's novel "problematizes the entire notion of the Left as a politicial stand. In its presentation of the relations between the Old Left and the New Left, neither wins the confrontation of generations; both are submitted to a serious critique that, in turn, paradoxically, gives them status and value" (Hutcheon 215). Probably no single work carries this Old Left legacy more memorably than Gold's *Jews Without Money* and no single writer is more implicated in it than Gold—"the best known Communist writer and critic of the time" (Gilbert, *Writers* 119), "the most famous representative" of "revolutionary sentimentalism" (Farrell 28–29). Moreover, *Jews Without Money*, like *Daniel*, articulates a poetics of left discourse for its readers: "There are enough pleasant liars writing in America. I will write a truthful book of poverty" (71).

Each work shares the assumption or at least the suspicion that such socialist materialism alone allows truthful representations of poverty (cf. *Daniel* 115–16). Each work, moreover, probes the assumption that religious Judaism has a genealogical bearing on modern socialism, especially on its more apocalyptic Marxist variants (Walzer 6, 134–35). As Paul Berman has suggested, in Gold's novel "Jewishness and socialism finally converge" (10). But where Gold seeks to integrate these not entirely compatible discourses—mostly in the hagiographic image of the narrator's mother (Dickstein, "Hallucinating" 162)—and to fashion a myth, Doctorow foregrounds the same messianic discourses as precarious fictions. Hence Daniel's admiration of his mother prompts historical inquiry, a genealogical analysis of her Communism in comparison to his "grandma's religion," which produces the generalizing designation of his mother as a typically "modern woman" (51). Doctorow's Daniel discovers divergence between his mother's politics and the grandmother's, whatever similar passions may underlie them, while Gold's narrator blurs this distinction. His mythic rendering of his mother, of her active maternal and marital solicitude and her reflexive championing of the oppressed, transforms her into an in-

stinctual Communist. Doctorow's immigrant mother—
Daniel's grandmother—curses impotently. By contrast, the
narrator's mother in *Jews Without Money* singlehandedly or-
ganizes rent strikes, effectively threatens duplicitous em-
ployers, nurses sick and brutalized tenement neighbors.
Her undifferentiating ministrations on behalf of gentiles as
well as Jews implicate her in Communist universalism
whereby proletarian solidarity displaces primitive, divisive
ethnic and religious affinities.

These differences between the two novels point to the
fundamental difference in rhetorical motive and ideological agenda. An unevenly realized aspiration to mythic authority governs Gold's work, while a resignation to its own
status as fiction informs Doctorow's self-referentially
open-ended "book." The way that both Gold and Doctorow appropriate a venerable melodramatic staple of protest narrative further underscores this distinction—between Gold's left myth and Doctorow's left fiction: Thus
each book recalls Dickens, whom Gold later honored
among the "subversive forces in my childhood that prepared me for socialism" (*Reader* 182). Daniel, however, dis-
parages his own life story as "David Copperfield kind of
crap" (117). At least since *Tale of Two Cities* a staple of both
revolutionary incitement and reformist indictment has
been the story of slum child run over by a wagon. Daniel
imagines a letter that his grandmother might have written
to a Yiddish newspaper in which she promises, "Oh I
could tell you stories." Such stories, however, never get
told. Instead they shrink into familiar story topics, the
common stock of *Ostjude* immigrant lore. Daniel's
Grandma Isaacson's catalogue includes the comic apocry-
pha of the greenhorn who forgot what he was supposed
to say when an Ellis Island official asked him his name and
so became an American under the incongruous name of
Ike Fergusson from the Yiddish *Ich vergissen* ("I forget"); a
harrowing recollection of drunken pogrom-crazed Cossacks; the incineration of siblings in the Triangle Fire. One
quick sentence in this obviously collective and thus dis-

missively generic history cursorily mentions a nameless child "crushed under a wagon" (79–80).

By contrast, the longest and climactic chapter in *Jews Without Money,* entitled "Blood Money," recounts in detail the death of the narrator's "sunny, loving" otherworldly sister Esther (274) on the world-darkening "miserable day of lead" (277–78) when a wagon ran her over. Confident that as a "proletarian realist" he could divorce melodrama and manipulative "straining" (*Anthology* 208), Gold elaborated the melodrama of Esther's death with a long twofold foreground. First he recalled the similar death of his boyhood friend Joey Cohen. The narrator has the bookish "dreamy boy in spectacles who was sorry when he killed a butterfly . . . sacrificed under the wheels of a horse car" just before first introducing Esther, "dancing[,] . . . flushed with joy in her ecstasy" (49–50). This introduction seems to read as a deliberate effort to prepare for the hyperbolic grief her killing provokes: "All the ghostly people began to cry. . . . Her eyes were shut, her face crushed and bloody. . . . My mother wailed. She tried to fling herself on Esther. . . . The little face was mutilated with deep wounds, as by a butcher's cleaver. . . . Father came from the bedroom and he howled like an animal" (280).

As the chapter title suggests, even this tragedy reinforces the novel's partisan moral, in the saintly mother's defiant refusal of cash—"blood money"—compensation from the company that owns the child-killing wagon (286). Here the mother's emphatic last word expresses inevitably sound "feelings" (286), at once conventionally maternal and (in Gold's view) politically correct. This convergence neatly corresponds to the anticapitalist animus of the narrator's Kulturkampf, at the expense of both the lawyer's apparent callousness and the father's bewildered, if pragmatic, ambivalence: "Maybe we should take the money. God knows we need it. . . . The child is gone, and nothing we do one way or the other makes any difference to our poor dove. So why——" The mother's one-word reply— "Silence!"—stifles all criticism and compels assent.

According to Frank Kermode, this motive and this re-sult—assent—distinguish myth from fiction. Both involve cultural politics and reflect writers' efforts to affect the discourses they inhabit and inherit. But, as Kermode invidiously contrasts myth and fiction, the motives for each form of representation are mutually exclusive: "Myth . . . presupposes total and adequate explanations of things as they are and were. . . . Myths are the agents of stability [and] call for absolute assent" (*Sense* 39).

Both messianic Judaism and party-line Marxism claim such mythic authority with their promised, redemptive inevitabilities—the coming of the prophesied savior and establishment of the absolutely egalitarian workers' state. William Empson (15–20) and James Gilbert (*Writers* 80) have noted the mythic, devotional desire governing professedly proletarian writing. In an early (1938) retrospective critique of proletarian fiction, Harold Strauss argued that such works invariably rest on myth (374). Exploiting the power of myth to "drive a man to action," Marxist writers had to move beyond simply demystifying "the mythology of the bourgeoisie," reducing it to its "material elements." Maxim Gorky encouraged mythmaking as a "romantic" supplement to "given reality" that "tends to provoke a revolutionary attitude" and so "changes the world" (qtd. in Williams 279). Advocating resistance to such mythography, Lionel Trilling found the ethics of myth and the decision to write either mythographically or in opposition to the assent-soliciting principle of myth particularly vexing for modern Jewish writers (*Speaking* 76). This vexation and the tension it produces enliven Gold's narrative until the very end, when Gold's narrator rejects the lesson of his own iconoclastic and demystifying narrative, the antimessianic skepticism that he exercised toward his Jewish heritage (Godine 206; cf. Rideout 188; Hicks 300). Malcolm Cowley has argued that Gold became increasingly committed to mythmaking in the years following *Jews Without Money* (*Think* 191–93).

This mythographic ambition has contributed, disproportionately, to the undue disparagement of Gold's work, both as an essayist and a novelist, as crude anti-intellectual agitprop. Such dismissals of Gold have obscured the import of *Jews Without Money* as fiction. In contrast to myths, fictions preclude assent and subvert total explantions: "Fictions are for finding things out, and they change, as the needs of sense-maing change. . . . Fictions are the agents of change. . . . Fictions [call] for conditional assent" (Kermode, *Sense* 39). Even when sympathetic critics discuss Gold's work as fiction, they often overlook its textual richness, its verbal density, its complex intellectual ambitions. Deferring the embrace of mythography and hence of univocality until the problematic end, most of Gold's narrative struggles where Salman Rushdie locates serious, politically responsive fiction "in the arena of discourse, the place where the struggle of languages can be acted out" ("Nothing" 110).

Gold's self-consciously oral style and the overall dialogic movement of his narrative place it in this arena. As much as its overt ideological concerns, this struggle makes it an apt precursor text to Doctorow's novel. Consequently, Daniel's citation of Gold is more than a suggestive illustration of the Isaacson's partisan singlemindedness. Both books' episodic structure and density, especially the strategic, orchestrating repetitions of suggestive sentences and phrases, further underscore their affiliation (Bakhtin 263). Consider, for example, the effect of Susan's refrain in *Daniel*, "They're still fucking us" (10, 19, 189) and Gold's narrator's defiantly self-deprecating attachment to "a gang of little Yids" (16, 36) or his father's resonant attachment— like Susan's—to a paralyzing grievance, his betrayal by "that thief, that Sam Kravitz (122, 100ff.). Such repetition, in each text, calls attention to the constructedness of the narratives, the embattledness of the narrators, and the contentiousness of their agendas.

Gold's express attention to his own phrases particularly runs counter to prevailing judgment of his crudity as a literary craftsman. It indicates that the contention in *Jews Without Money* is not simple partisan animus and ideological assertion but rather dialogic contestation. Thus the clash of voices and sounds—laughter, cursing, singing—with which the novel opens coalesces dialogically as "the great carnival or catastrophe" (14). Gold achieved this effect—critical counterpointing of ideological stances—throughout *Jews Without Money*. In chapter 10, the jingoist doggerel in praise of Washington, which Gold's narrator learned in school and recites in a wine cellar at his drunken father's urging, is framed with a comic Talmudic dispute and a disruptive brawl over money between the narrator's father and a kinsman (119–22). In the rapid succession in chapter 19 from an awkward profession of love (rendered as dialogue) to a declamation on behalf of labor unions, which the narrator truncates, to a summarily reported "orgy of talk," the pressures and pleasures of dialogic contestation become even more pronounced (236–39)

The way these books implicate themselves in and foreground available rhetorics of apocalyptic redemption—Jewish messianism and revolutionary Marxism—further reflects the affiliation between the two novels. The shared agenda includes efforts to enact a left critique as narrative in recognition of the greater authority and appeal of stories (cf. *J* 22, 82–84) over didactic polemics and "stuffy schoolmasterly" essays (Fussell, *Abroad* 204–5). Gold and Doctorow also appropriate the mythic, syncretic ground of Jewish radicalism. Occupying much of this ground, they appeal to the cliché that assimilating Jews have traditionally exploited in winning over their gentile compatriots. Such conquests, however, tend to be partial, as Edmund Wilson's grudging assent to this cliché illustrates:

The Jew lends himself easily to Communism because it enables him to devote himself to a high cause, involving all of humanity, characteristics which are natural to him as a Jew—he is already secretive, half alien, a member of an opposition, a member of a minority at cross purposes with the community he lives. . . . The Jews have the sense of the revolt of the industrial workers in the cities—they have no sense of the American revolutionary tradition. (*Thirties* 379)

Hence the narrators of both *Jews Without Money* and *Daniel* repeatedly stress their narrators' "Americanness," in knowledge as well as temperament. This emphasis produces an anxious recognition and a reactive internalization of Wilson's demurral about radical Jews' deficient "Americanness." Thus Daniel's appropriative deformation of Patrick Henry echoes the parrotlike schoolboy declamation on Washington by Gold's narrator. Recognizing this effort on Gold's part, Marcus Klein argues that *Jews Without Money* is as much an effort to Americanize its narrator (*Foreigners* 190, 235) as it is an exposé of poverty and an incitement to revolution. According to Klein, Gold strove to make Jewishness, Americanness, and revolutionary Communism compatible, to invoke "an avenging socialistic Messiah who looked like Buffalo Bill" (192).

Each work, Gold's and Doctorow's, enacts a dialogic encounter—dogmatically shut down in *Jews Without Money* and never completed in *Daniel*—between the two Jewish discourses of justice and redemption, modern secular socialism and traditional religious messianism (cf. Rideout 152). Moreover, each author grounds this encounter in an American vulgate that encompasses baseball, TV, Buffalo Bill, saloons, immigrant Pidgin English, swearing, public school indoctrination. In Doctorow's novel these discourses converge, only to come apart under the pressure of Daniel's analysis (250). Part of what feeds this analysis derives from Daniel's encounter with Artie Sternlicht, a New Left Yippie Svengali who serves as a guru to Daniel's sister Susan (163–72, 185–92). The account of Sternlicht contrasts pointedly with Daniel's grudgingly respectful memories of his parents' defense counsel, Jacob Asher (143–46), who dominates some of the most emotionally demanding scenes in the novel (21, 178, 198). Asher's doubly allusive and cruelly ironic biblical name evokes the failure of providential hope inasmuch as it couples the name of the Jewish founding father Jacob, when he was preparing to give his divinely designated new name, "Israel," to both a chosen people and their promised land, with the surname Asher. This second name retracts the promise in the name Jacob, in recalling the least legitimate son of Israel who, generations later (in Judges), gave his name to a tribe of cowards. This self-canceling naming underscores Daniel's divided judgment of the lawyer as embodying the "Jewish" worship of justice that turned so many first-generation American Jews, like Daniel's parents and like Mike Gold, to Communism:

For Ascher, my parents' Communism was easily condoned because it was pathetic and gutsy at the same time . . . the large arms of ethical sanctity he could wrap around an atheistic Communist when in the person of a misfit Jew as ignorant as my father. . . . Ascher understood how someone could forswear his Jewish heritage and take for his own the perfectionist dream of heaven on earth, and in spite of that, or perhaps because of it, still consider himself a Jew. (146; cf. Hook 88)

Doctorow also endows Artie Sternlicht with an etymologically ironic name. Daniel's observations reinforce this irony. Artie indeed seems "arty," in the derogatory sense that connotes bohemian dilettantism. In his self-aggrandizing, charismatically irreverent oral delivery, Sternlicht also appears starlike as the English translation of his German name insists—so much so that Daniel introduces Sternlicht as the subject, or star, of a *Cosmopolitan* feature. Daniel even signals his scorn for Sternlicht with the observation that Sternlicht's apartment contains only three furnishings—a color TV and an unfinished collage, reminiscent of both Rauschenberg and Warhol, along with a mattress on the floor (166, 186).

Sternlicht's pop apocalypse and hip messianism can't stand up to Asher's moral rigor, the dialogic contestation between reformist skepticism and messianic longing that he endures and embodies. This tension also resounds in Doctorow's plagiarized title and is reinforced in his first epigraph, a quotation from the original "book of Daniel." Thus accrediting Asher's troubled and compassionate wisdom, Doctorow opposes his "Daniel" to *the* original book of Daniel—the late Aramaic Old Testament work that uneasily transformed a redemptive captivity narrative into an apocalyptic prophecy.

Doctorow's express affiliation with Gold seems to rest

largely on their shared will to prophesy. Even though he has Daniel deprive traditional biblical prophesy of its apocalyptic urgency, Doctorow, like Gold, seeks to recover such prophetic authority and, recognizing its limitations as a form of knowledge and its deceptive lure as rhetoric, to adapt it to secular ends—"a revoicing of moral outrage" on behalf of democracy (Callahan 257–59). Cornel West has recently elaborated on this Emersonian program of "prophesying man-making words" as "prophetic pragmatism," an egalitarian, iconoclastic critique on behalf of "social change" (232–33). Drawing on the "political relevance of the biblical focus on the plight of the wretched of the earth," this pragmatism "harks back to the Jewish and Christian prophets who brought urgent and compassionate critique to bear on the evils of their day."

For all the prophetic pragmatism that Daniel articulates—in his lectures on state violence, his retrospective indictment of Cold War mind control, his evocative recollection of mob violence—traditional biblical promises of deliverance finally have no more authority for Daniel than do Sternlicht's shallow promises of love and revolution. As a student of history, Daniel believes no promises; as a narrator he makes no promises. This antimythic absence of promises and refusal of certainties in *The Book of Daniel* indicate the most obvious difference between Doctorow's novel and Gold's precursor work, while the fostering of "prophetic pragmatism" makes for an even more decisive affiliation between them.

Though Gold's essays during the 1920s before the publication of *Jews Without Money* demonstrate his commitment to prophetic pragmatism, he enacts his commitment to prophecy most emphatically, though not uncritically, in *Jews Without Money*. V. F. Calverton's praise of its "biblical simplicity and candor" reflects this balance (463). Thus the opening passage introduces a prophet who stands in both an archaic "natural" biblical space and in a modern media-made "cultural" space as he steps out of "whirlwinds of dust and newspapers. The prostitutes laughed shrilly. A prophet passed, an old-clothes Jew with a white beard.

Kids were dancing around the hurdy-gurdy. Two bums slugged each other" (14).

In Gold's typescript, this image of the prophet goes further. After introducing the prophet's stereotypical "white beard," Gold continued his description: "sad, mysterious, eternal in a crushed derby hat. He patiently bore a bundle on his back. He heard the organ play, 'Hot Time in the Old Town Tonight,' but plodded on. Only the hearts of his American descendants leaped to the tune" (2).

Gold at once dignified this prophet with the three adjectives and then disconnected him from his milieu, his "American descendants" and their (musical) mass culture. He thus established the value of prophecy and the need to adapt to New World circumstances. The more severe and succinct published version depends on readers' inferring the gravity and majesty of the traditional-looking "white bearded" prophet, qualities the typescript spelled out in adjectives, thus stressing the prophet's displacement. In contrast to Gold's typescript, the published version shows traditional prophecy as even more imperiled than did the earlier version.

In addition to a critical commitment to prophecy, both Gold and Doctorow employ remarkably similar means in articulating divergent, though perhaps equally subversive, discourses. Each novelist's picaresque first-person narrator presents himself as cultural rummager and iconoclastic *bricoleur* who pays close attention to texts, images, and icons of his own local—family and neighborhood and dissident—cultures and representations of the larger mainstream culture. Each writer also stresses conflicts among such representations. As V. F. Calverton observed in the 1920s, such culture clash—exposing it and provoking it—is what distinguishes revolutionary writing (Gilbert, *Writers* 80).

# 2 Caliban and the Police

Winston woke up with the word 'Shakespeare' on his lips.    —George Orwell, *Nineteen Eighty-Four*

In the name of all dissonance, what can it be?
    —Nathaniel Hawthorne, *The House of Seven Gables*

Despite persisting claims for *Jews Without Money* as a classic, as "a seminal text of the Depression years" and as "a prototype setting the pattern for succeeding novels" (Dickstein, "Tenement" 67; Fiedler, *Jew* 30), there is little consensus as to what kind of book it is: is it a novel or an autobiography? Gold encouraged his publisher, Horace Liveright, to market it as nonfiction. (The college library where I work has it catalogued as sociology.)

Not necessarily a fault, this generic uncertainty results from a tension between the struggle the book enacts and the conclusion it reaches. *Jews Without Money* makes its overt claims as an affirmative conversion narrative, an account of the narrator's emergence from ghetto parochialism and self-seeking individualism to enlightened revolutionary Communism in the form of "the worker's Messiah." But what most readers find compelling in *Jews Without Money* is at odds with the book's didactic, apocalyptic closure. The most discerning readers ascribe its resonance and rhetorical authority to its evocative, sometimes documentary immediacy (Rideout 151, Godine 205, Dickstein, "Hallucinating" 159–60). The many voices that Gold's narrator evokes rather than the one he ultimately privileges make his book memorable. Though lacking narrative coherence, Gold's "many voices" associatively produce a singular cogency (Folsom, "Book").

Following the lead of critics such as Folsom, Rideout, Godine, and Dickstein, I set out in the preceding chapter to reinforce this consensus by establishing the authority of *Jews Without Money* as a precursor text in a radical canon and by demonstrating Gold's dialogic management of voices. I also pointed out in chapter 1 that the first individual voice we hear in Gold's novel belongs to a cursing parrot. The terse announcement that "a parrot cursed" (13) sets the rhetorical agenda for the entire book and establishes the narrator's stance as a Kulturkampf warrior. This agenda consists, according to Michael Folsom, of "building a counter-culture . . . creating and sustaining . . . anti-establishment cultural institutions" ("Education" 229, 231). The culture war that *Jews Without Money,* like Gold's less well-known criticism and sketches, enacts serves this effort and characteristically turns on the opposition between received representations and perceived material circumstances. Thus Gold opened his narrative with an image of a cultural tradition adapted for commerce and with explicit attention to act of interpretation. He concentrated these concerns in a close-up shot of a neighborhood prostitute wearing "a million dollars worth of paste diamonds" on "her fat fingers" and "a red kimono decorated with cherry trees, mountains, waterfalls, and *old philosophers* . . . eating an apple . . . with the dignity of a whole *chamber of commerce* at its annual banquet. . . . We scampered around her in a monkey gang. We yelled at her those words whose *terrible meaning* we could not fully guess: 'Fifty cents a night!' . . . She spat like a poisoned cat" (17; emphasis added).

Other animal imagery in the opening pages—in addi-

tion to a cursing parrot, a poisoned cat, a monkey gang—
reinforces this Kulturkampf agenda: "The saloon goat lay
on the sidewalk and dreamily consumed a *Police Gazette*"
(14). Obviously and comically, this goat exhibits the critical
outsider's hunger for culture that characterizes proletarian
writing of the thirties, from Gold's *Jews Without Money* to
Richard Wright's *Black Boy.* Thus the narrator of *The Disinherited* by Jack Conroy recalls: "We were starved for
print. . . . I have never overcome the habit of stooping
down to capture every vagrant circular or stray newspaper
that I encounter" (21). The print hunger Conroy ascribed
to his disaffected proletarian narrator recalls a similar lex-
ophilia pervasive in New York's Jewish ghettos. In the earliest popular American ghetto Bildungsroman in English,
Abraham Cahan's David Levinsky remembers how, as a
result of constant newspaper reading, his "pocket was always full of all sorts of clippings" (269).

A comic displacement of a widespread and apparently
generic ghetto culture hunger, Gold's goat also embodies,
conversely, the resistance to official culture, high and low,
that pervades *Jews Without Money.* In both respects this
goat serves as an authorial surrogate, performing two obvious acts of political and cultural criticism. First this image recalls how the police, throughout Gold's work, stand
synecdochically for repression and hegemony. In 1924,
Gold implicitly equated New York's literary establishment
with the city's Tammany-run police force; thus cops appear
in *Jews Without Money* as cowardly, complacent, beer-
guzzling, and thieving (24, 44–45) as do the literati in
Gold's earlier commentary: "In New York the careful writer
always carries a handful of fine cigars and kind words
about him for the critics [who] are like the police force of
literature (*Anthology* 120). Over a decade later, when Gold
himself had taken to policing culture on behalf of his embattled party, he set out to examine and lament the "police
character" of the "renegade" writers who had followed
Leon Trotsky out of the Communist party (Kempton 11).

Gold's goat not only chews, swallows, and thus effaces
*Police Gazette* accounts of police bravery and intelligence.

In doing so, this goat at once enjoys and destroys one of the more prevalent mass culture opiates of Gold's New York boyhood. *The Police Gazette* at that time served as the "barbershop bible" and mainstay of barroom discourse. Flamboyant and titillating, with its pink pages, burlesque queen profiles, prize fight gossip, "sex scandals, sex pictures, sex advertising," the *Gazette* also earnestly upheld the status quo in its editorial pages, celebrating the supposed probity of state and private-sector virtue enforcers—city cops, railroad bulls, Pinkertons, Texas Rangers, etc. (Mott 329–31; Schiller 98). More obliquely, Gold sustains this critique of the press with his image later in the book of a dirty melting snowman reading a newspaper with "amazed eyes and idiotic grin" (242). Gold's work as a media critic continued throughout the thirties, marked by frequent celebrity bashing: of Shirley Temple (*CW* 169), of "sycophantic tales" about J. D. Rockefeller (138), of the orchestrated solicitude for Lindbergh's baby (172), of that "suave young Harvard genius" Walter Lippmann "embarking on his remarkable career of opportunism" (140), and, especially, of the Hearst press (*CW* 83, 146, 227). Gold's correspondence with Freeman reveals that Gold was at work on a play savaging Hearst during much of the mid-thirties. Freeman recalls that, as a reporter in the twenties, Gold wrote in deliberate opposition to mainstream "bourgeois journalism" (*AT* 252).

As surrogate culture critics, Gold's goat and parrot share the burden of authorial commentary between them. The goat gets the easier job of attacking exploitative, obviously hegemony-sustaining mass culture. But the cursing parrot from whom readers first hear has the harder and more important task—speaking for the ghetto—since Gold's narrator reminds us three pages later that the first thing ghetto Jews do when they gather on the street "to talk" is "to curse" (16). Consequently, the cursing parrot reappears a hundred pages later, reinforcing the importance and the difficulty of cursing in Gold's Kulturkampf. As early as 1924, Gold identified the "curse" and "blasphemy" with the rhetorical repertory of the "thoroughly experienced prophet" and went on to equate "blasphemy and criticism" (*Anthology* 120).

In *Jews Without Money* the narrator's father sarcastically appoints the foul-mouthed parrot to the post of rabbi, the doctrinal and ceremonial authority among observant Jews. The ironic equation of the parrot's curses with the presumably high-minded prayers of the pious and the suggestion that cursing belongs in a sanctuary for tradition and spirituality reveal the centrality of cursing for Gold, given Gold's stress on prophecy (see chapter 1).

Even old Mrs. Fingerman's parrot talked more than other parrots. Mr. Fingerman had been an invalid for years, and his one distraction before he died had been to teach his parrot to curse in Yiddish.

My father laughed heartily.

"What a good Jew that parrot is!" he said. "He can curse and he hates Christians! I am sure that we will find this parrot in the synagogue next Saturday leading our prayers." (113)

Even more revealing is the narrative sequence framing the father's praise for the cursing parrot. With this mordant recollection of the Fingerman parrot the narrator ironically digresses from a rhapsody on the verbal freedom, the exuberance and the witty volubility of ghetto Jews. Apparently a celebration of "the great joy of the Jewish race, great torrents of boundless exalted talk . . . the baseball, the golf, the poker, the love and war of the Jewish race" (112–13), the rhapsody turns sardonic with the resonant cursing of the Fingerman parrot, a surrogate voice of embittered impotence, whose owner's dimunitive name as well as his immobilizing condition bespeak an emblematic helplessness. The narrator cannot sustain his celebration because his rhapsody is markedly dissonant from the circumstances that occasioned it. The substance of the remembered conversation belies the exaltation with which the narrator remembers it (111–12). By introducing this cursing parrot as the representative voice of ghetto-bred rage, Gold undercuts his young narrator's rhapsody before it begins.

The narrator's father, who alternates throughout the book between the despair rendered here and Micawber-like optimism, began this chapter—"A House Painter's Tears"—cursing. "Why must I work at his accursed trade? . . . A curse on Columbus! A curse on America, the thief! It is a land where the lice make fortunes and the good men starve!" (112).

This curse, *"ein klug tsu Columbus,"* was a stock phrase in the ghetto volubility that Gold's narrator tries to celebrate, a curse that Jewish writers from Gold to Philip Roth took pains to unpack (Klein, *Foreigners* 189–90; Pinsker 10–11). In *Jews Without Money,* Gold stressed the priority of cursing in ghetto discourse and helped establish its value as a literary resource. As illustrated in my reading of Doctorow's *The Book of Daniel,* such cursing has become a commonplace in American Jewish writing, a means of inscribing the rage of the have-not in a more ostensibly dispassionate, intellectual, even analytic cultural critique. Samuel Sillen has detailed Gold's career-long concern to wage such a Kulturkampf. "He led the battle for a true people's culture whose outlines he sketched as early as 1920" and, by the end of the decade, scored "a knockout blow" with his controversial attack on Thornton Wilder (Gold, *Reader* 10–11). In the forties, Gold attacked "Wall Street monopolists [who] cocked their revolvers at [the] WPA cultural movement" (*Anthology* 253), while, in anticipation of the Wall Street Crash, he lamented the emergence of a "crap-shooting bourgeoisie [as] the 'new' audience for art" (*Reader* 52).

Gold's work in the early twenties reveals a marked tension between his longing to participate in established culture and the rage articulated as a curse on its moral bankruptcy. Thus Gold opened his apprentice manifesto "Towards Proletarian Art" by acknowledging this strain: "We are prepared for the economic revolution . . . but what shakes with doubt is the cultural upheaval that must come" (*Anthology* 62). A year later, Gold's urgent desire to be initiated and his realization of his exclusion appear in an early autobiographical sketch entitled "The Password to Thought—to Culture." It tells of a garment worker in his early twenties, a Lower East Side Jew, who only wants to read—mostly Ruskin—and isn't allowed to, either at home or at work. " 'What are you here for anyway, to work or to stuff yourself with fairy tales? . . . What do you want with culture and thought, anyway?' the boss cried waving his cigar like an orator. 'Me and Mr. Shinster was worse off than you once; we started from the bottom; and look where we got without sesames or lilies! You're wasting your good time, boy! . . . David spat viciously at the door that closed behind him" (102–3). The story ends seconding the mute curse that the youth's spitting here expresses, acknowledging the need to curse, with Gold's alter ego "stung by anger," about to curse or "speak sharply" to his mother, an impulse he resists out of weariness (110).

Gold's legacy, helping to establish cursing as cultural critique, resurfaces in Philip Roth's evocatively titled first novel *Goodbye Columbus* and in the Yiddish resonance of its narrator-protagonist's name, Neil Klugman. This name links a homophone of "kneel," which hints at defeat, with the Yiddish echoes of the surname Klugman. *Klug* can mean either "curse" or "clever" (Landis 165). Though these characteristics mark Gold's prose, Gold's reputation has exaggerated the rage and obscured the cleverness and artistry. According to Alfred Kazin, rage—the "urgent release" of anger—constitutes Gold's entire contribution as a writer (*Native* 387).* Kazin's censure, however, evades the exacting rhetorical challenge that rage poses for writers seeking to express it. Kazin resists recognizing the extent to which cursing may be the most venerable, psychically satisfying, and even self-empowering rhetorical form for rage to take (Hartman 130–32).

In *Jews Without Money* such cursing has a decided, consistent polemical cast. It defies prevalent myths of America as the "new world" that Columbus discovered or as a

---

*Fifty years later Kazin tempered this judgment in describing *Jews Without Money* as "an eloquent but primitive outpouring of emotion" in "The Art of *Call It Sleep*," *New York Review of Books* (October 10, 1991), pp. 15–18.

promised land that European Jews and Cambridge-edu-
cated Puritans alike expected to reach at the end of their
respective exoduses. The wide stylistic and ideological
gulf between Gold and Philip Roth may suggest the appeal
and the authority of cursing as a critical gesture and a
trope of defiance among warily assimilated Jewish American writers. This defiance centers on a discovery of the
persistence of exclusive, antimeritocratic hierarchy. Hence
both *Jews Without Money* and *Goodbye Columbus* reject an
affiliation with elite culture and the schooling that certifies
this affiliation. Consequently, *Goodbye Columbus* closes in
Harvard Yard with Neil Klugman poised, after his Rad-
cliffe girlfriend jilts him, to "pick up a rock and heave it
right through the glass" window of Lamont Library (96).
Klugman, who will now return to his job as a shelving
clerk in the Newark Public Library, had briefly penetrated
the expensively educated Brenda just as, fleetingly, in the
thirties, Gold's "Marxism penetrated all the ivory towers"
(*Anthology* 291). In both cases the desire to penetrate and
appropriate mixes tellingly with the compulsion to conquer, to assault and perhaps to vandalize American culture's most notable monuments to its own magnificence.
" 'Trotsky' was Trotsky's jailer's name," Salman Rushdie
writes and "by taking it for his own, he symbolically con-
quered his captor and set himself free" ("Pen" 54). Such
appropriative moves pervade Gold's writing.

Both Roth and Gold mine a venerable tradition of literary Harvard bashing. It includes Ishmael's boast in chapter
24 of *Moby-Dick* that "a whaleship was my Yale College and
my Harvard" and, insider status notwithstanding, Henry
Adams's intimately observed conclusion that "all Harvard
College taught . . . was [the] absence of enthusiasm" (68).
Less obliquely, Gold opened a sketch he wrote soon before
composing *Jews Without Money* with the following dis-
claimer: "Certain enemies have led the slander that I once
attended Harvard college. This is a lie. I worked on the
garbage dump in Boston, city of Harvard. But that's all"
(*Anthology* 177; cf. Folsom "Education" 225–27).

In Gold's myth, Harvard stands for more than social
and economic "schoolboy" privilege (Gold, *HM* 10; Hof-

stadter 293). It stands for "the bourgeois monopoly of literature" that, in waging culture war, Gold strove to overthrow (*HM* 27). In "Love on a Garbage Dump," Gold's relocation of Harvard (from Cambridge to Boston) recalls the extent to which Gold, throughout his work, concerned himself with the genteel cultural privilege traditionally associated with Boston—and, misogynistically, with "schoolmarmish" women. Gold also exploited Philip Rahv's "redskin" commonplace in *Jews Without Money,* where "the old maid teacher . . . bade us admire Nature" (40; cf. *Reader* 148; Rahv, 1–5). Gold's contemptuous dismissal of Edmund Wilson as "a Beacon Hill matron" underscores this animus (*Reader* 11). Such a repudiation comes decisively at the end of *Jews Without Money* when Gold's narrator finishes grammar school and parts with a genuinely solicitous English teacher.

"It would be a pity for you to go into a factory. I have never seen better English compositions than yours, Michael.

"I must work, Miss Barry," I said. I started to leave. She took my hand. I could smell the fresh spring lilacs in the brass bowl on her desk.

"Wait she said earnestly. I want you to promise me to study at night. I will give you a list of the required high school reading: you can make up your Regents' counts that way. Will you do it?"

"Yes, Miss Barry," I lied to her sullenly. . . . I had always loved books. . . . Since I couldn't, I meant to despise all that nonsense.

"It will be difficult to study at night," said Miss Barry in her trembly voice, "but Abraham Lincoln did it, and other great Americans."

She presented me with a parting gift . . . a volume of Emerson's Essays. (304–5)

The narrator reports that he "threw the book under the bed when I got home and never read a page in it, or in any book for the next five years" and that he "hated books" because "they were lies, they had nothing to do with life and work."

To the extent that he serves as an autobiographical alter ego, Gold's narrator "lies" or at least contradicts the *propria persona* Gold, who repeatedly honored Emerson and his legacy in his political-literary commentary (*Anthology* 295;

*Reader* 142; Foslom, "Education" 250–51). This contradiction does not hinge on any inherent characteristic of Emerson's but rather on the political use that has been made of his legacy and on the immigrant reaction to that use. Joseph Freeman described the literary conditions under which he and Gold came of age as a time when "literature was the enemy of the street" during the years before "postwar fiction gave the language of the street the dignity of art "(*AT* 17). Irving Howe recalls that even a generation later

American romanticism was more likely to reach us through the streets than the schools, through enticements of popular songs then the austere demands of sacred texts. We absorbed, to be sure, fragments of Emerson, but of an Emerson denatured and turned into a spiritual godfather of Herbert Hoover. . . . The whole complex of Emersonian individualism seemed . . . a device of the Christians to lure us into a gentility that could only leave us helpless in the worldly struggle ahead. ("Thirties" 22–23)

While it would be as pointless to try to find the "real" Gold among these incompatible positions as it is to find the "real" Emerson among Howe's, such appropriations do point to Gold's complicit mastery of the high culture he so often reviled, and perhaps to the inevitability with which Caliban must become Prospero in order to pursue his program of defiance.

This animus especially marks Gold's agitation on behalf of Sacco and Vanzetti in "Lynchers in Frockcoats," an indictment of Massachusetts governor Fuller and Harvard president Lowell as "idealists who religiously read Emerson and live on textile mill dividends," the "degenerated" heirs to "the proud old libertarian tradition of Abolition" (*Anthology* 151). The resentment underlying this animus resonates sarcastically in *Jews Without Money* when the narrator confers Mayflower pedigrees on himself and his Chrystie Street neighbors: "Every tenement home was a Plymouth Rock" (73).

Notwithstanding his antagonism, Gold's traditionalist nostalgia exposes an affiliative identification with the cultural heritage labeled the American Renaissance as much as it censures products of that heritage. Throughout Gold's work, the same heritage that Gold denigrates sets the standard for cultural vitality and integrity. Gold hastened, in 1941, to pronounce his own prime as a writer, the thirties, a "second American Renaissance": "The Thirties compares favorably with the Civil War decade, the greatest single chapter in the history of American culture"—a "Golden Age" rivaled only by the thirties (*Anthology* 291). Similarly, he recalled "the gathering of young genius" at the Provincetown Playhouse in 1916 "such as America had not seen since Concord" (*Reader* 159). In a late autobiographical essay Gold even ascribes his socialism to the American Renaissance and especially to the abolitionist "struggle against slavery" (*Reader* 181, 183).

Here Gold's identification of the Civil War as primarily an abolitionist struggle rather than a nationalist struggle for the Union illuminates Gold's recurrent, lifelong appropriations of Lincoln—whom American Communists fighting for the Spanish Republic in 1936 honored by naming themselves the Lincoln Brigade (Klein 89; cf. Gold, *Reader* 180)—and more notably of John Brown in Gold's canonsetting lists. These honor rolls—of writers and freedom fighters with whom Gold sought to affiliate himself and his agenda—recur throughout his essays.

John Brown, Thomas Jefferson and Abraham Lincoln were among those present in Union Square when the clubbing began. (*Reader* 56)

It is the spirit of the Revolution that works and ferments in Trotsky, as it once fermented in Danton, Voltaire, Shelley, Blake, Walt Whitman, and John Brown. (*Anthology* 132)

Gold exploited the propriety of this practice among mainstream literati in his autobiographical apologia, "Why I Am a Communist." There Gold recalls inhabiting—much like David in "The Password to Thought—to Culture"— "the idealistic world of Shelley, Blake, Walt Whitman, Kropotkin" (210). In his 1938 essay "Marxism and Literature," Edmund Wilson accounted dismissively for this appropriative practice, for its value to the literary left: "The prescribers for the literature of the future usually cherish some great figure of the past whom they regard as having fulfilled their conditions and whom they are always bringing forward to demonstrate the inferiority of the literature of the present. . . . They are obliged to provide imaginary versions of what their ideal writers are like" (*Triple* 280–81).

Gold practiced such appropriation in his very first book. Published in 1923, this biographical tribute to John Brown presents him as a revolutionary prophet armed and recalls Thoreau's 1859 eulogy. In 1936, Gold and Michael Blankfort adapted this tribute for the stage, allusively retitling it "Battle Hymn." In the earlier work, Gold seemed to be composing at once a covert autobiography and a plan for his own revolutionary career, the career of someone who had a more credible claim on the culture he was challenging—seeking to seize—than those who owned it. Hence Gold, who adopted a Civil War veteran's name to replace his native name of Izthok Granich (*Reader* 181), dwells on Brown's Pilgrim and revolutionary pedigree (Brown 10) and on Brown's status in the Emerson-Thoreau-Alcott Concord set (42). Gold also celebrates the biblical, distinctly Old Testament sublimity Brown projected as a Puritan Samson (5, 55). Gold's attention to Brown's unimpeachable "Americanness"—to both the sacred Puritan and secular republican strains of Americanness—covertly transforms Gold's prosaic immigrant marginality, as one of the "huddled masses," into a promise of heroism, an intimation of the virility of Old Testament warriors like Gideon and Joshua, an assertion of the authority of angry prophets like Jeremiah. Written at about the same time as "The Password to Thought," Gold's John Brown biography places Brown in the autodidact tradition of Lincoln, Franklin, and Douglass, stressing "how John Brown educated himself"—how he "read passionately" though denied, like Gold, any advanced schooling (13).

Moving Brown as beau ideal of the American manhood to which Gold aspires, a model of revolutionary courage and prophetic grandeur, even closer to home, Gold introduced "August Bondi, a brave and able young Austrian Jew" who served under Brown's leadership" (35). Bondi appears here not only as one of Brown's Liberty Guards, but also as a chronicler of Brown's campaigns, "a soldier who has studied history" (*Anthology* 139). As a writer, a worker in resonant words as well as martial deeds, Bondi assumes one of the chronic stereotyped attributes of the Jewish immigrant. In the twenties Gold identified his scholar-warrior beau ideal with Trotsky, heir to Brown's "revolutionary spirit": "The best general and tactician in Europe. . . . reads and writes five or six languages . . . finds time to turn out at least two important books a year (*Anthology* 131–32).

After Trotsky became anathema in the late twenties, Gold turned to Isaac Babel for an ideal of bookish militance (*Anthology* 234). The Ukrainian Jew, who fought in a Red Cossack regiment during the civil war that followed the Russian Revolution, evoked that struggle in *Red Cavalry*, among the most lasting fiction to come out of the Russian Revolution. According to Lionel Trilling, Babel's stories characteristically turn on the opposition between Cossack ideals of virility, even savagery, and clichés of Jewish bookishness and timidity. Babel's sense of irony that he, as "an intellectual, a writer . . . with spectacles on his nose and autumn in his heart," rides into battle as a Cossack revolutionary governs this opposition (Babel 19–20).

Gold addressed the problem of Jewish bookishness throughout his career. At his crudest, Gold's presumption of militance made him one of those literary Marxists Edmund Wilson ridiculed as "pursuing a literary career under the impression that they are operating a bombing-plane" against Franco (*Shores* 650). Approaching this matter ethnographically as well as autobiographically, Gold both acknowledged and undermined the widespread view of Jews as "a timid bookish lot" whom America "has taught to kill" (J 37).

In "The Writer in America," a 1953 autobiographical reminiscence, Gold speculated: "maybe there were subversive forces in my childhood that prepared me for socialism. The New York Public Library, for instance. I was an ardent reader" (*Reader* 183). Notwithstanding Gold's fond recollection of the New York Public Library, the left Kulturkampf that Gold championed targeted museums, libraries, and Ivy League colleges as emblems of oppressive cultural hegemony. Gold's ironic views of New York City's major libraries in his 1921 account of "the American Famine" demonstrate this antagonism to institutional culture and to "the police of literature" (*Anthology* 120): "Oppressed . . . sad outcasts under the sheltered entrances to the Cooper Union Library. They were in the reading room, scores of them, gazing like slow-witted kine through the endless pages of the meadow-wide newspapers" (*Anthology* 91). Uptown at the Astor Library, Gold found "a bunch huddled under a noble statue of William Cullen Bryant, poet of calm and serenity. In the library reading rooms we found dozens of others, prowling about disconsolately, too distracted to read" (192). Gold's infamous homophobic attack on Thornton Wilder as "prophet of the genteel Christ" and "poet of the genteel bourgoisie," unleashes a series of exasperated metaphors damning his work. One of them identifies the "museum" with a "historic junkshop" (199; cf. *HM* 52).

An instructive elaboration of this metonymic assault appears in a book often paired with Gold's *Jews Without Money* in discussions of proletarian writing and literary Communism, Henry Roth's 1934 novel *Call It Sleep*. Roth devotes a chapter to a Metropolitan Museum visit by his boy protagonist David Schearl and his decidedly and defiantly unrefined (spitting and armpit-sniffing) immigrant Aunt Bertha (147–51). Walking from the Third Avenue Elevated to Fifth Avenue, "runneling" terracing "the bosom of her green dress" as she "cursed" the July heat, she becomes an iconoclastic commentator when they arrive at the museum; Roth punctuates the entire visit with Bertha's curses. "Kiss my arse," she tells the Italian peanut vendor who gives them directions. "A plague on you! . . . May your heart burn the way my feet are burning!" she mutters toward the couple she adopted, without their knowing, as museum guides. She prefaces her departing malediction by spitting on the steps, "May a bolt shatter you to bits! If I ever walk up these stairs again, I hope to give birth to a pair of pewter twins!" As a response to Bertha's superlative crudity, "David began to feel uneasy at his aunt's loud voice and her Yiddish speech both of which seemed out of place here." David's sense of his place and of his own lack thereof resonate in Bertha's comic failure to recognize the authority and appreciate the historical meanings—let alone value the grandeur—of the museum's contents. Consequently, she reacts incredulously and viscerally to a work that most readers, like most museum goers, would recognize immediately as a depiction of a familiar classical myth—Romulus and Remus nursing:

Wherever their two unwitting guides strolled, his aunt and he tagged along behind. Now and then, however, when she was particularly struck by some piece of sculpture, they allowed their leaders to draw so far ahead that they almost lost them. This happened once when she stood gawking at the spectacle of a stone wolf suckling two infants.

"Woe is me!" Her tone was loud enough for the guard to knit his brows at her. "Who could believe it—a dog with babies!"

Since fashionable museum goers are usually more restrained, Bertha's susceptibility and enthusiasm, which the guard's frown censures, seem as "out of place" in this cultural preserve as Bertha herself. Her more worldly, more assimilated brother-in-law, David's sullen father, affirms this exclusionary judgment: "A raw jade like you ought to learn a little more before she butts into America!" In protorevolutionary rage, Bertha retorts with a sarcastic and proverbial curse on culture and, implicitly, on Columbus: "My cultivated American," she asks. "How long is it since you shit on the ocean?"

Over the course of his long writing career, Gold took a stauncher anticulture stance than Roth who—unlike Gold—never worked as a full-time party polemicist and who renounced his youthful Communism in his middle years (Klein 194). Gold aimed to overcome the proletariat's persistent, disabling "reverence for book culture" (*Anthology* 76). But in making this effort, Gold built much of his irreverence and iconoclasm on the "book culture" he assaulted; he transformed his own youthful cultural reverence into a compelling curse on culture. Here perhaps lay "the password" that his autobiographical antagonist despaired of learning.

Consequently, the counterculture animus underlying Gold's and much of the left's ongoing polemical curse on culture draws on the high-culture stature and power of cursing, on its long reputable literary pedigree (Ramazani 170; Hartman 130). Even Coleridge, the most eminent and probably the most discerning reactionary in English letters, divided human speech between prayers and curses ("Fears in Solitude"). The canon-bound cursemaker to whom Gold owes the most, William Blake, also belongs to the Romantic poetic inheritance that Gold, for all his insurgence, never could repudiate. Repeatedly including Blake on his canon-making lists, Gold praises Blake's "great stormy music of Anglo-Saxon speech" and his commitment—like Trotsky's—"to work for a better world" (*Anthology* 200, 139). But the most striking affinity lies in Blake's subversive recasting of Jesus as a master curser whose blasphemies were blessings: "This is the race that Jesus ran: / Humble to God, Haughty to Man, / Cursing the Rulers before the People / Even to the temple's highest steeple" ("The Everlasting Gospel" 1. 67).

Gold effusively praised Blake's seditious curse on England: "Blake poured forth mystic dithyrambs of revolution, and was arrested and tried for sedition for wearing a red liberty cap in the street, and saying in public he wished the Revolution would come to England, to purge that gross land" (*Anthology* 130). Gold's appropriation of Blake's more lyric voice informs a chapter of *Jews Without Money* entitled "Did God Make Bedbugs?". Here Gold's narrator's questions to the rabbi echo the catechistic voice of "The Lamb" and "The Tyger" (cf. Retamar 46). Gold not only cursed throughout *Jews Without Money*; like Blake, Gold's narrator paid especial attention to "the Harlot's curse." The sexual blight of Blake's "London" "blooms" as well on Chrystie Street—New York's "red light district" in Gold's recreated boyhood (14–17, 25–34, 75–76, 267).

Gold's attention to the curse, his apprehension of the rhetorical value and even the literary status of cursing, gives his narrative a resonance beyond the left Kulturkampf that Gold led. Despite Gold's populist agenda, this resonance is distinctly literary, canonic, and high-culture. It looks backward, toward library-enshrined classics, as much as it looks forward to an egalitarian utopia, and to *Goodbye Columbus* and *The Book of Daniel*.

The classic, library-enshrined writer Gold alludes to, discusses, and appropriates most notably throughout his fiction and his criticism is Shakespeare. In Gold's criticism, Iago stands for both literary philistinism (*Reader* 163) and for "nay-saying" Trotskyist intellectuals (*Anthology* 266). An exchange in "The Password to Thought—to Culture" illustrates Gold's awareness that Shakespeare, the way his works have been understood, is a perennial focal point for cultural contestation and an unavoidable battleground for American Kulturkampf contestants. The factory owner asks the autobiographical protagonist two questions: "What do want with thought and culture anyway?" and "Do you ever read Shakespeare?" (*Anthology* 103). Then he launches into a lecture, a reductive amalgam of Babbitt and Polonius, in defense of status quo inequality:

Well, ye know in Choolyus Caesar, this man Caesar says: Let me have men about that are fat, and that don't think; that is, don't think outside of business, ye understand. Well, that's my advice to you, my boy, especially if ye want to hold your job and got any ambition. The last feller that held your job was made a salesman on the road after five years, and the same chances are open to you. Now let's see whether you're smart or not. . . . Now let's see you use common sense after this—not Thought and Culture.

(Notice especially how Gold, echoing Mark Anthony, ironically stressed "ambition" after introducing *Julius Caesar*.)

A striking Shakespeare passage in *Jews Without Money* draws on *The Tempest* and recalls the most notable curseutterer in Anglo-American literary tradition, the monster who called the "red plague" down on his oppressors: the immigrant miser Fyfka whom Gold's narrator renamed "Caliban" is "tortured . . . by a horrible conflict between body and mind" (76). This Caliban, however, never speaks, unlike Shakespeare's, who has warned or inspired centuries of cultivated readers as to the power of subjugated expression: "You taught me language, and my profit on't / Is, I know how to curse. The red plague rid you / For learning me your language!" (1.2.363).

Gold's other reference to Caliban also shows him wordlessly expressive, "roaring rather than speaking" (*Reader* 15). In order to evoke the "gloom" and "cruelty" in the lives of urban factory workers, a decade before *Jews Without Money*, in an article entitled "American Famine," Gold identified Caliban as a tamed monster: "The elevated roared; Caliban rushing on the errands of man." In *Jews Without Money*, Gold implicitly elaborated this conceit in the narrator's account of a family excursion, by elevated train, to the Bronx. Here mass transit embodies the conditions that provoke "cursing."

The train was worse than a cattle car . . . crowded with people to the point of nausea. Excited screaming mothers, fathers sagging under enormous lunch baskets, children yelling, puking and running under everyone's legs, a gang of tough Irish kids in baseball suits who persisted in swinging from the straps—sweating bodies and exasperated nerves—grinding lurching train . . . a hundred bodies battered into each other, bedlam of legs and arms, sneezing, spitting, cursing, sighing—a super-tenement on wheels. . . . My father cursed each time a fat wet matron flopped in his lap or trod on his corns. (150)

The stress on cursing, here and elsewhere in the book, helps account for Gold's interest in Shakespeare's monster. This interest suggests that he saw his calling as a revolutionary writer in giving voice to Caliban and, by doing so, in making Shakespeare speak to and for the masses Gold claimed to represent. *The Tempest*, according to Stephen Greenblatt, stands out in Shakespeare's corpus as an enactment of Kulturkampf. Showing an encounter between a cultivated "European whose sole source of power is his library and a savage who had no speech at all," Shakespeare raised questions of authority that "for a modern audience . . . center on the figure of Caliban ("Curse" 568; *Negotiations* 157).

In view of Gold's interest in the figure of Caliban, Caliban's place in New York cultural life during Gold's apprentice years seems suggestive.

The major event in celebration of the three hundredth anniversary of Shakespeare's death . . . celebrated in New York in 1916 [was] a ten-day run of an extravaganza entitled *Caliban by the Yellow Sands*, written by the poet Percy MacKaye, and performed by a cast of over 1,500 actors, singers, and dancers in Lewisohn Stadium before a total audience of 135,000. This *Tempest*-like allegory concluded with Caliban, who has yearned to usurp Prospero and rape Miranda, kneeling at the feet of a God-like Shakespeare. (Levine 80)

Levine's account doesn't note the extent to which MacKaye's misreading of Shakespeare subdued Caliban in the way that Widow Douglas sought to "sivilize" a good-natured Huck Finn. MacKaye's preface establishes this intention quite plainly:

Caliban, then, in this Masque, is that passionate child-curious part of us all [whether as individuals or as races] groveling close to his aboriginal origins, yet groping up and staggering . . . toward that serener plane of pity and love, reason and disciplined will, where Miranda and Prospero commune with Ariel and his Spirits. . . . The theme of the Masque—Caliban seeking to learn the art of Prospero—is, of course, the slow education of mankind through the influences of cooperative art.

Clearly, MacKaye's recasting of Caliban serves a politics of social control. In 1866, George Eliot had Felix Holt warn that "while Caliban is Caliban, though you multiply him by a million, he'll worship every Trinculo that carries a bottle (Eliot 369). Such sentiments informed the genteel and effete liberalism that had become "the reigning creed of the educated classes" by 1916: "Men could be best con-

trolled and directed not by the old crude method of force
but by 'education' in the broadest sense" and by "adjust-
ment" (Lasch, *New* 146). In MacKaye's masque, the "airy
spirit" Ariel has a legion of subordinate "spirits" who
speak the last lines. Shakespeare's original, by contrast,
gives the restored, overtly empowered Duke Prospero the
last word. This difference suggests the extent to which
MacKaye's work affirms both a politics of social control and
the genteel evasions whereby such control masks its own
force and effect. In opposition to MacKaye's apparent
hegemony-maintaining agenda, Gold's mute Caliban represents a twofold challenge that transgresses MacKaye's
more uniform agenda: "to learn the art of Prospero," Caliban's enslaver, in order to usurp Prospero, as the original
Caliban intended.

An oblique indication of Gold's contempt for the patrician liberalism dominant in the teens and reflected in
MacKaye's masque appears in *Jews Without Money* in the
narrator's ironic treatment of Teddy Roosevelt as a hege-
monic icon and subject for "art." In his best and most ad-
mired friend Nigger's home—a "dingy gaslit" sweatshop-
apartment where seven people share three rooms with a
chamberpot, toys, newspapers, pieces of cloth and tailor's
trimmings—on "a poisonous green wall" hangs "a chromo
showing Teddy Roosevelt charging up San Juan Hill; the
most popular art work of the period" (262). Much earlier
in the book, entirely without irony, Gold's narrator noticed
the same "chromo" in a public (as opposed to private)
space, the Rivington Street wine cellar where his father
and his landsmen gathered. "Under a big American flag,
hung a chromo showing Roosevelt charging up San Juan
Hill" (115). Thus by dint of repeated attention to this ido-
latrous "chromo," marveling at first and sarcastic at last,
Gold establishes Roosevelt—Veblenesque scion of New
York's Anglo-Dutch merchant elite, Groton- and Harvard-
bred wielder of the "big stick" against small countries,
subduer of dark-skinned Asians and Latinos, legendary
island conqueror, sponsor of the Great White Fleet, eloquent master of the "bully pulpit"—as the icon to match

his iconoclasm against, as a Prospero to be challenged by Gold's insurgent, articulate Caliban.

Whether or not Gold actually saw MacKaye's masque, its status as a major middle-brow hit during Gold's literary apprentice years is a measure of widespread interest in Caliban at the time. Moreover, MacKaye's mugwumpish defeat of Caliban, his denaturing and demeaning appropriation, clearly affirms prevailing hierarchies just as the masque's popularity establishes resoundingly who—still—owns Shakespeare, who owns "culture." Perhaps no writer more strikingly embodied these hierarchies and the alliance of class privilege, wealth, and cultural authority that Gold spent his adult life defying than did Percy MacKaye. His impeccably genteel tradition credentials include hereditary affiliation with New York high culture (through his father, Steele MacKaye, a prominent playwright, designer, and impressario). MacKaye worked as a Manhattan prep school teacher after schooling at Harvard and in Germany. A retrospective attachment to a secure static literary canon pervades his works, which include an adaptation of Hawthorne's "Feathertop" for the stage, a libretto based on "Rip Van Winkle" (which Gold also adapted for the stage seven years later as *Hoboken Blues, or the Black Rip Van Winkle*), verse-dramas entitled "The Canterbury Pilgrims," "Jeanne d'Arc," and "Sappho and Phaon."

MacKaye's cultural affiliations bear close resemblance to those of the literary patricians of Gold's own generation whom Gold savaged during his years as an arbiter of the literary left (Lasch, *Agony* 51–52). Gold's 1930 attack on Thornton Wilder is his most remembered performance as a critic and as an "aesthete-baiting" Caliban (*Anthology* 197–203; Castronovo 14). It is also his most influential, according to Edmund Wilson, who recounted how Gold's attack touched off a "literary class war": "This assault provoked one of the most violent controversies which the literary world has lately known" (*Shores* 534–39; cf. Aaron 258–60; Klein, *Foreigners* 244–47). Gold's attack established literary Marxism as a serious stance and the counterattack it provoked marked "the eruption of the Marxist issues out of the literary circles of the radicals into the fields of general criticism."

In savaging Wilder—a "rape" according to Hart Crane—Gold was ostensibly reviewing Wilder's novel *The Woman of Andros*, which he "based upon *The Andria*, a comedy of Terence, who in turn based his work upon two Greek plays . . . by Menander" (from Wilder's headnote). Since even favorable reviewers found Wilder's novel "slight" (Simon 75–76), the resonance of Gold's attack must lie elsewhere; it lies in what David Castronovo, a sympathetic Wilder biographer, judges the "cultural importance of Gold's remarks" (14–15):

Today, Gold seems like the literary muscle of the Communist Party, someone ready to enforce the standards of the gang on the independent artist. But in 1930 the attack looked different: Gold was a respected figure in the movement whose integrity was rarely questioned and whose book, *Jews Without Money*, exposed a side of American injustice. Wilder, by contrast, had recently made a great deal of money by presenting the agonies of materially comfortable people; he was undeniably genteel—second-generation Yale, restrained in speech and manner . . . a target for an adversary looking to make social style the criterion for literary worth. . . . That [Gold's] characterization is crude does not prevent it from being potent.

Gold's assumption of Caliban's voice in opposing genteel hegemony became more pronounced during the thirties, the period when the cultural populism of the left had grown most influential—most threatening to the genteel tradition. Despite his own prominence and authority during this period, the "heyday" of "proletarian literature" in America (Nelson 164), Gold continued to single out Ivy League patrician writers for vitriolic attack.

The same age as Gold, Archibald MacLeish graduated from Yale and enrolled at Harvard Law School at about the same time that Gold became a union organizer in Boston, met Bartolomeo Vanzetti, and realized that he couldn't afford to study at Harvard even though he had been admitted. MacLeish's career came to be marked by a tension between his blue-chip background and achievement—as a Pulitzer poetry laureate, charter editor of *Fortune*, Librarian of Congress, FDR adviser—and his outspoken commitments to economic equality and early anti-Fascism. Such leftist sympathies made MacLeish "the most famous case of a poet falling in and out of favor" with the briefly dominant literary left in the thirties (Nelson 162). Troubling himself with the "conflict about the relation between art and politics," MacLeish moved Gold to charge that MacLeish's poetry "exhibited a 'fascist unconscious'" and to label him "Der Schöne Archibald," representative of "white-collar fascists out of Harvard and Wall Street" (Nelson 162; Aaron 283). At the close of the decade, when Gold began to savage fellow travelers, party "renegades," and Trotskyite "lackeys," MacLeish counterattacked in *The Irresponsibles* against his assailants and against "the revolution of our age" with which he had once been earnestly sympathetic: "Caliban in the miserable and besotted swamp," according to MacLeish, "is the symbol of this revolution" (15–17).

According to Daniel Aaron, Lewis Mumford "extended MacLeish's liberal counterattack" against the totalitarian convergence that crystallized in the Hitler-Stalin alliance and their 1939 invasion of Poland (283). Mumford's role here as a liberal anticommunist Kulturkampf combatant involves more than a doctrinal disputation with Gold, since Mumford and Gold grew up together as novice literary radicals and Village bohemians (Miller 96–101).

Of the dozen or so young men who passed in and out of this small group . . . Irwin Granich, who later became Michael Gold, was one of the most promising literary talents that was ever sacrificed to the petrified dogmas of Russian Communism. In his original anarchist phase, so much closer to his natural disposition, it was Gold who brought me a copy of "Shropshire Lad" to read aloud on one of our walks. (Mumford, *Sketches* 135; cf. Gold *Anthology* 269).

Looking back on this culture struggle between his values and Gold's, Mumford identified the object of his invective as "the uprising of Caliban," who came to personify the demoralizing forces of modern barbarism" (*Interpretations* 334, 339). "Promoted by a complacent naturalism and a misapplied egalitarianism" that diminished Prospero, Caliban's most lasting triumph, according to Mumford, was the establishment and spread of Soviet Communism, which falsely "promised justice and equality."

Despite their obviously pejorative intent, MacLeish's diatribe against Caliban and Mumford's judgment on Gold, Communism, and Caliban are all measures of Gold's success. As Gold forged his identity as a revolutionary, he "frantically fashioned for himself a self-image" as a "class-conscious child of the tenements" (Cooper, 159). He exhibited an everyday affinity for Caliban. In Max Eastman's account: "Mike was a dark-eyed handsome social mutineer with wide lush lips, uncombed hair, and a habit of chewing tobacco and keeping himself a little dirty to emphasize his identity with the proletariat" (*Love* 265). Joseph Freeman, Gold's associate over two decades, regarded Gold's Caliban persona as a calculated performance:

He affected dirty shirts, a big black, uncleaned stetson with the brim of a sombrero; smoked stinking, twisted Italian three-cent cigars, and spat frequently and vigorously on the floor—whether the floor was covered by an expensive carpet in a rich aesthete's studio or was the bare wooden floor of the small office where Gold's desk was littered with disorderly papers. These "proletarian" props were as much a costume as the bohemian's sideburns and opera cape. (*AT* 257)

The sombrero brim in Freeman's reminiscence hints at how much Gold's defiant and apparently entertaining identification with Caliban informs his articulations on matters of race and nationality as well as his more immediate, more personal, more dogmatic concern with class. "Two Mexicos," Gold's emblematic *Liberator* story from 1920, illustrates this concern. Here a landowner notable for his "dark, stern Indian features," who "wanted to turn [his] entire ranch over to" his tenant farmers and who stands for "the goodness that is in Mexico," confronts his paler, dissipated, English-speaking brother in a quasi-apocalyptic revolution-portending showdown (*Anthology* 61, 52–54).

Here and elsewhere Gold presaged recent attention to representations of European imperialism and the suffering it produced. Appropriations and politically challenging readings of Caliban as a rebellious colonial subject, bearer of subjugated knowledge and legitimate claims for justice, have pervaded interest in *The Tempest* since the 1960s (Fiedler 209, 230, 248; Retamar 13–16; Vaughn 289–90). An index of Gold's engagement with the plight of Caliban, as we now understand him, is his 1940 report on a visit to Puerto Rico. Here Gold attacks the policy of schooling Puerto Ricans "in English, the tongue of the master" and so insidiously "producing colonial subjects" (*Reader* 103).

A similar agenda, advocacy for Caliban, informs Gold's attention to domestic racial oppression. Gold worked over a twenty-year period with the leading African-American figures on the cultural left, including Claude McKay, Paul Robeson, and Langston Hughes (Gold, *Reader* 188; Duberman 107; Rampersad 335, 338). In 1935, Gold described the common ground between Yiddish culture and "Negro spirituals" as "the hopeless melancholy of poverty" (*Anthology* 226). Looking back from the forties, Gold noted, with some justice and much pride, that the proletarian literary movement of the thirties had made an unprecedented effort to integrate American letters "with Negro workers displaying for the first time the full humanity, the tragic courage and simple, sober, self-respect and unquenchable aspiration of the Negro people" (*HM* 48):

No American author of any quality can find it in himself any longer to show the Negro as a strutting clown. The cliché has been shattered forever, outside of Hollywood and the *Saturday Evening Post*. And for this enormous new perception, this lifting to human dignity of the Negro people, to whom give thanks but to "Moscow-dominated, party-dictated" pioneers of proletarian literature in the Thirties?

A futurist and constructivist account of a Harlem man's pursuit of prosperity, Gold's 1927 play, *Hoboken Blues, or the*

*Black Rip van Winkle*, works as a sort of anti-*Tempest*. The New Jersey city named in Gold's title stands sardonically for a delusive utopia—Miranda's brave new world, Gonzalo's peaceable polity—across the water from Harlem. In this mythic Hoboken "everybody's happy all the time" (576). The play moves between a familiar, historical Harlem and this projected Hoboken utopia, which, when actually encountered, imposes even more constricted and oppressive conditions than Harlem itself. In one Harlem scene, Gold showed the relationship between words and power or, in Caliban's terms, learning language and the "profit" on it. One character, a corrupt but "respectable" Harlem business man—a mortician and failing hustler—ridicules his wayward son by stressing his failure to learn proper English, to master the master's language: "Oswald, I's ashamed of you. Ah give you de best education money could buy, Eton collars and embalming and religion, but you're a failure. Dat odder press agent wuz weaving circles around you with his language. You don't even know language, you don't" (617).

Such passages, like several in *Jews Without Money*, show how much critical irony and dialectical skepticism inform Gold's sympathy for the marginal and oppressed—African-Americans as well as Jews—and thus Gold's advocacy on behalf of Caliban. As Michael Folsom observes, complaints about Gold's sentimentality are overstated and self-serving inasmuch as they divorce sympathy and action, a divorce Folsom judges disablingly self-congratulatory on the part of Gold's critics ("Book"). According to Folsom, Gold's urgent association of language and action moots such objections because it precludes conventionally sentimental effects—vicarious self-righteous indignation combined with complacent passivity.

This imperative even underlay Gold's choice of names, his own and his fictional characters'. "Mike Gold" (taken from a Civil War veteran Gold knew as boy), though more "American" than Itzhok Granich—Gold's native name—remains distinctly Jewish and at the same time, at least in Gold's private mythology, has a martial resonance that serves as a summons to fight for liberation (*Reader* 183). In *Jews Without Money*, the most provocative instance of Gold's imperative of wedding sympathy and defiant—if not revolutionary—violence occurs in his naming, and his rendering, of the most daring, the most defiant, and perhaps the most oppressed character in *Jews Without Money*. The character who embodies the strongest will to action also suffers the most abysmal, Caliban-like childhood in the novel (261–67). Provocatively, Gold named this character "Nigger," even though he is only another "Jew without money" like the narrator himself (42). In "Why I Am a Communist," Gold recalled his realization of the need to complement his growing revolutionary consciousness with a deliberate will to act, even to provoke and endure violence (*Anthology* 210). This 1932 manifesto describes how Gold and his friends "formed a Red Guard of about a thousand youths in New York" to go fight for the Bolsheviks in Russia. This essay recalls the jauntiness of Gold's descriptions in *Jews Without Money* of the street gangs that Nigger formed and led, "a gang of little Yids" (42–43) and later "the Young Avengers" (260). The narrator's judgment of Nigger as "the bravest of the brave, the chieftan of our brave savage tribe" and as a champion of his weaker, more timid "tribesmen" shows readers Caliban resurgent, a revolutionary in the making. Moreover, the figure of a Jewish "white nigger" doctrinally advances Communist internationalism, which holds racial and ethnic differences to be incidental, except when capitalist hegemonists reify such differences to mask the only fundamental social difference, class.

Gold's provocatively resonant naming in *Jews Without Money* foregrounds minor characters like Fyfka/Caliban and more central characters—like Nigger—who at once endure and resist oppression. Gold's set-piece description of Fyfka the Miser—the character actually renamed Caliban—reveals a grimmer side of the Caliban condition. This passage also shows a tension that marks Gold's entire narrative. It shows the narrator divided between deliberate rhetorical control and mastery of his culture's code—

his literariness—and the rage and urgency of populist agitprop. This division results in a materialist account of the making of Fyfka, the miserly Caliban, and of his pathology (74–76). Despite widespread views of Gold as an intellectually crude party-line propagandist, his perverse dialectic in this passage frustrates any facile left sympathy for Caliban as an object of exploitation or as an emblematic victim of oppression.

Before identifying Fyfka as a Caliban, Gold's narrator presents him an unwelcome boarder in his family's apartment. Fyfka never pays rent and saves all his sweatshop wages by subsisting daily on three rolls and "a three-cent slice of herring" and then "like a dog" mutely begging supper from the narrator's family with his "dumb, gloomy, animal face." Then the narrator transforms this pathologically self-denying miser into a libidinous wild man, a sexually crazed "Caliban . . . tortured, behind his low puckered brow by a horrible conflict between body and mind." After reminding the reader (as he does throughout *Jews Without Money*) that his street was "a red light district," which "waited for this Caliban's body's peace," the narrator recalls how "the miser watched the busy women night after night until he could endure it no more" and how "the madman . . . wanted a woman, but was too stingy to pay the regular price of fifty cents."

Gold here tempts the reader to blame this miser-madman for his own misery, only to confront us with the complicitous effect of our language in the making of such Calibans. Thus the animal imagery that recurs throughout this passage recalls the vocabulary that has traditionally sanctioned and maintained invidious class distinctions and colonial subjugation. The random melange of animals associated with Fyfka—dog, ape, baboon, maggot—precludes any single authoritative or definitive description of Fyfka; thus Gold disables by excess the language whereby hierarchies produce invidious taxonomies and disguise them as natural and scientific. In doing so, he raids the means whereby language masters, Prospero as scientist or narrator or official apologist, represent and thus produce "lower orders" so as to subjugate them. Thus the narrator's diagnostic notation of Caliban's "low puckered forehead" may allude to a related subjugating discourse, phrenology. This popular pseudoscience served, throughout the nineteenth century, to sanction "natural" class and colonial hierarchy (Levine 221–22).

For all his bestial monstrosity, Gold's Caliban is distinctly human insofar as avarice is solely a human, socially produced trait. He lacks the appealing noble savagery of the narrator's friend Nigger or of Caliban figures in more conventionally sympathetic left representations of him. Moreover, this monstrous miser lacks even the ambiguously tragic grandeur of the Shylock miser myth. Jacob Riis, the most influential liberal ethnographer of Gold's ghetto, explained such stereotypically miserly Jewish immigrants by eruditely ascribing their condition to "an avenging Nemesis" (107). In contrast to the pacifying dignity in Riis's image, Gold's narrator shows the ghetto miser as a "thing . . . a human garbage can of horror." The ostensibly impartial passive voice with which the narrator expressly introduces Fyfka as Caliban—"was tortured"—reinforces this reduction. The context and sequence of this "human garbage can" image, though, preclude easy acceptance of Fyfka's condition—as "garbage"—as innate or essential or natural. This image belongs to a cumulative list of alternative or complementary descriptions of Fyfka. Transformations of Fyfka include changing him from "thing" to "ape" to "fevered Rothschild in a filthy shirt; madman in an old derby hat." The last two images insist that Fyfka is a social product, with both a historical role model in Rothschild and ironically status-conferring clothing—his worn derby.

Though a minor character in a set piece that interrupts his narrative, Fyfka/Caliban appears at a crucial juncture in *Jews Without Money,* immediately after the narrator intrusively states the overall agenda of the book, "to write a truthful book about poverty" (71). Within five pages, the narrator introduces Fyfka with a sweeping thesis statement: "Poverty makes some people insane." Poverty, a social condition, makes Calibans—and Shylocks—and Gold here evokes this conditioning. In fact, the very title of this chapter, "The Miser and the Bum," in its seeming accept-ance of familiar categories of behavior, indicates Gold's own concern with the production of social types. Examin-ing this production, Gold shows how capitalism (as he understood it) moots questions of individual character that so exercise bourgeois readers and writers. Hence the im-perative that introduces Caliban instructs readers simulta-neously to rely on and to transcend what we think we know of social types: "Imagine the *kind* of man this Fyfka the miser was."

Gold's appropriation of Caliban and Caliban's preroga-tive, cursing, not only serves his analytic and polemic Marxist agenda. It also established Gold's claim to speak for the culture he opposed; American literary culture has grounded itself in exactly the sort of insurgence Gold solic-ited and, more particularly, in the perennial contestation over Shakespeare that Gold practiced. In American literary history, claims to Shakespeare date at least as early as Cooper's pronouncement in 1828 that Shakespeare is "the great author of America." Subsequently, Melville, Poe, Twain, and Whitman called for—some envisioning them-selves as—a distinctly American Shakespeare (Levine 70; Orvell 4).

Beyond appropriating Caliban, Gold also made several more explicit claims to Shakespeare. The narrator in *Jews Without Money* recalls how ghetto "garment workers lived with Shakespeare" (88). Gold's sexagenarian reminiscence, "A Jewish Childhood in the New York Slums," includes effusions over "the glorious Yiddish theater" where as a boy he came to know "the divine Shakespeare, playwright of all humanity . . . marvelous Shakespeare, who despite his own prejudice, could yet register some of the deeps of Jewish tragedy" (*Anthology* 310–13). Irving Howe cites a report that the first Yiddish performance of *Hamlet* in New York prompted the audience to call for its author (*World* 466).

Whether prompted by Emerson's progressive cultural nationalism or Gold's "change the world" revolutionary internationalism, such gestures seem governed by Orwell's insight that to control the past is to control the future. These appropriations and identifications suggest the extent to which Gold's attention to Shakespeare indicates an effort to participate, institutionally and historically, in American literature. Hence Gold's most influential manifesto, "Proletarian Realism," published the same year as *Jews Without Money*, defiantly echoes Melville's self-promoting tribute to Hawthorne and Emerson's various summonings of the American literary hero-genius. Just as Melville warned not to look for a Shakespeare dressed in Elizabethan costume, so Gold asked:

Who could expect a Walt Whitman at the court of Louis the Fourteenth? Bourgeois intellectuals tell us, there can be no such thing as a proletarian literature. . . . Then they say it is mediocre; where is your Shakespeare? And we answer: Wait ten years more. He is on his way. We gave you a Lenin; we will give you a proletarian Shakespeare, too; if that is so important. (*Anthology* 204)

Gold reconstructed a familiar conversation here, familiar in both American literary history and in current culture wars, whether in Sydney Smith's belittling 1820 query, "Who reads a book by an American?" or, more recently, in Saul Bellow's vain, contemptuous search for "the Zulu Tolstoy." Moreover, Gold's archly conditional clause at the end of the quoted passage shows how well and how warily he recognized the familiarity of such hegemony-contesting exchanges and the extent to which Shakespeare provided an expedient banner in such culture clashes. As Kenneth Burke recalled: "When the Leftists first moved onto the scene I began to fear that they were dishonoring Shakespeare. For a couple of years there, I took all sorts of notes for articles in defense of Shakespeare. Then all of a sudden I made the discovery: 'Look, this fellow has been taking care of himself for a long time'" (Aaron, "Symposium" 500).

In the attack on Wilder, the most decisive crisis in Gold's Kulturkampf, he offered a protoproletarian Shakespeare (who happens to resemble Gold as Freeman and Eastman described him) as a challenge and corrective to the literary gentility Wilder represented. The genteel WASP owner-ship of Shakespeare had eviscerated his language, turned it "archaic and inaccessible" as in MacKaye's masque (Lev-ine 80). Thus Gold opposed Wilder's "neat, tailor-made rhetoric . . . to the great stormy music of Anglo-Saxon speech," insisting that "Shakespeare is crude and dis-orderly beside Mr. Wilder" (*Anthology* 200). Then, with an easy sarcastic allusion, Gold established that—as an American, as a Jew, as a salt-of-the-earth proletarian—he owned Shakespeare more than the Yale WASP Wilder. Mocking Wilder's style, Gold voiced his own affinities for Shakespeare and for Shylock: "Prick it, and it will bleed violet ink and *aperitif.*"

Such salt-of-the-earth "Shakespeares in overalls" are nothing new in British and American culture wars (Aaron, *Writers* 222). Even before Melville pictured Shakespeare in "Hawthorne's Mosses" as a Kentucky woodsman, and be-fore the king and duke in *Huckleberry Finn* comically man-gled Shakespeare's loftiest lines, Samuel Johnson honored Shakespeare's plainspoken earthiness. As a reproach to arid academism, Johnson's "Preface to Shakespeare" casts Joseph Addison in much the same role that Gold assigned Wilder: they "speak the language of poets" while Shake-speare—and presumably Johnson and Gold—"speak the language of men." Johnson's metaphoric contrast of styles opposes a regular, orderly, correct garden to a wild, end-lessly diverse forest. "He that will understand Shake-speare," Johnson concluded, "must not be content to study him in the closet, he must look for his meaning sometimes among the sports of the field, and sometimes among the manufactures of the shop."

The very familiarity of Gold's self-empowering situating of Shakespeare among "machinists, sailors, farmers, weavers," in "Proletarian Realism," and Gold's recasting of Shakespeare as a protoproletarian further suggest Gold's subversive mastery of the culture he challenged (*Anthology* 203–6). Gold's mastery, implicit enough to be covert, belies Richard Hofstadter's charge that Gold, in his role as party "hatchetman . . . had succeeded more fully than most left

intellectuals in declassing and deintellectualizing himself"
(293–95). Hofstadter's dismissal reflects a limited understanding of what intellectuals do (Said 81). This view con-
fines intellect to "the power of ideas" or, as Roberto Retamar observes, it limits Ariel to "serving Prospero" rather
than "allying himself with Prospero in his struggle for true
freedom" (39). This kind of understanding has operated
institutionally and thus restrictively within the universities
and professions that produced and maintained the very
monopoly that Gold and his comrades waged their Kulturkampf against (Bender 317, 393, 246; Jacoby 84).

Close attention to Gold's writing reveals, contrary to
Hofstadter, an overreaching and venerable *intellectual* ambition. As Michael Folsom argues, Gold "did not foreswear
his commitment to the life of the mind . . . but rather revised it in a way which the custodians of our culture can
scarcely conceive" (Education" 229). Like Caliban, Gold set
out "first to possess [Prospero's] books." Rather than
"deintellectualizing" himself and his Communist position,
Gold's canonic appropriations, allusions, and commentar-
ies represent an effort to wrest literary production from its
academic monopoly and the hierarchies that this monopoly supports. Gold's appreciation of how susceptible language and culture are to monopoly power surfaces in a
deleted passage in the typescript of *Jews Without Money*.
Here the narrator remembers: "My mother never told stories; that was my father's monopoly" (114). This observation recalls, critically, the narrator's generous recollection
earlier, in chapter 7, of his father's narrative gift as well as
his defective sense of intellectual property and of the
means of its production. This chapter, "The Golden Bear,"
ends by recounting the father's failure as an impressario,
as a would-be marketer of ideas and texts, to appropriate
and take commercial advantage of his idea for a theatrical
production of Schiller's play *The Robbers*. Gold's allusiveness here pits the father's Romantic hopelessness, the
counterrevolutionary defeatism that Schiller's tragedy affirms, with the narrator's own apocalyptic and revolutionary Romanticism, which corresponds to the narrator's
Blakean voice (Abrams 195; Folsom, "Education" 250).

Neither a debasement of intellect nor an endorsement of illiteracy, Gold's raids on established cultural monopolies—particularly the Shakespeare franchise—resemble what Houston Baker identifies as Caliban's play and describes as "supraliteracy . . . guerilla action carried out within . . . territories of the erstwhile masters" (384). Such action consists of using dense, literary language that the "masters" recognize only as "crude hooting." Henry James, in a famous recollection of a visit to Gold's Lower East Side, rehearses Prospero's reaction to Caliban's play. "The brooding critic" James arrives on behalf of English-language literature, "astride of the consecrated English tradition" to meet "the dragon" of an "alien presence" (138–39):

It was in the light of letters, that is in the light of our language as literature has hitherto known it, that one stared at this all-unconscious impudence of the agency of future ravage. . . . One's "lettered" anguish came in the turn of one's eye from face to face for some betrayal of a prehensile hook for the linguistic tradition as one had known it. . . . In this chamber of present urbanities . . . the critic's ear . . . could still always catch, in the pauses of talk, the faint groan of his ghost. . . . The East Side cafes . . . showed to my inner sense . . . as torture rooms of the living idiom; the piteous gasp of which at the portent of lacerations to come could reach me in any drop of the surrounding Accent of the Future. The accent of the very ultimate future, in the States, may be destined to become the most beautiful on the globe and the very music of humanity (here the "ethnic" synthesis shrouds itself thicker than ever); but whatever we shall know it for, certainly we shall not know it for English—in any sense for which there is an existing literary measure. (138–39)

Playing the ironic prophet, James heard the sounds with which ghetto-bred ethnic proletarians like Gold would construe dissonance and wage Kulturkampf. The "hoot" that, according to Baker, the masters hear—and hear only—or the groans and gasps that James heard recall the animal traits Gold ascribed to his tortured Caliban, Fyfka the Miser, a failed monopolist ("a fevered Rothschild") like the narrator's theatrically-inclined, storytelling father.

Dissonant sounds such as James pondered and Baker privileges open *Jews Without Money*, most notably those of a cursing parrot. Along with a lexiphagic goat, Gold rendered this parrot as a successful intruder in the city of man—as an "other" in current critical parlance. Thriving among alien humans, these two animals appropriate human language in ways that can prompt various responses from their human masters: dismiss their utterances and gestures; overlook them as it may be too easy for Gold's readers to overlook his agenda—and so deny its intellectual content (as did Hofstadter in reaction to Gold); respond with disdain yet fascinated curiosity (as did James).

Reviewers of *Jews Without Money* did all of the above. Some reviews attest to Gold's mastery of the "supraliteracy" that Baker describes, and to Gold's success in invading and transcending colonizing discourse (382). Gold's book satisfied the most conventional standards. The reviewer for the *New York Times* legitimated Gold's book by associating it with acknowledged past masters, recalling "the deep shadows of a Rembrandt picture and the high challenge of a Whitman poem" (BRD 1930). The same reviewer, obviously reflecting the prevailing Eliotic disdain for the merely personal, hastened to reassure readers that Gold's book "surpasses autobiography" (despite Gold's insistence to his publisher, Horace Liveright, that he sell the book as autobiography). The reviewer for the *World* seconded that "Gold has written with profound feeling and sometimes with fury, but he has never lost control of his own emotions." Even a reviewer who faulted Gold for violating Eliotic strictures of impersonality praised Gold's "curious, compelling power." Another praised the sincerity and authority of "enduring qualities" in Gold's narrative. This same writer, though, insisted that Gold's "revolting" book "smells of the sewer," while the reviewer who linked Gold to Rembrandt conceded that the book "offends good taste" and that Gold's "English is not always the

King's." This divided praise, for literary artfulness and for material directness, points to the effect and perhaps the transcendence toward which Kulturkampf art strives— what Baker calls Caliban's "invasion" of the dominant discourses.

Edmund Wilson described a distinctly Marxist effort "to transcend literature itself" (*Triple* 289). Gold's language-using animals or human "primitives"—the parrot and the goat, Nigger, the bestial miser, and the Caliban persona that Gold himself assumed as a critic—all share and serve as Gold's surrogates in the effort Wilson described. They all represent an aspiration, "beyond literature" or culture, for the "transcendent realm" Kenneth Burke described as "a realm of things in themselves" (*Grammar* 191). While Gold's goat eats words and the parrot makes sounds, both indifferent to their meanings, Caliban finds in language only one thing—one function, one motive—cursing. Such transcendence downward can balance extremes of iconoclasm and hagiography while promising eventual redemption (Burke, *Attitudes* 337). But such transcendence cannot initiate, let alone fully produce, any material change in the quality of Caliban's lives. Here, according to Burke, lies the impasse that any intellectually thoroughgoing Marxist or "dialectical materialist" inevitably faces.

The Kulturkampf that Gold enacted in *Jews Without Money*, which much of Gold's other writing promotes, arrives at such an impasse. Gold's success and the success of the left in the thirties in sharing, if not fully seizing, the means of cultural production never resulted in the transformation they envisioned. As a Communist Caliban or as an American Shakespeare, Gold faced the impasse that, Michel Foucault insisted, obstructs every Kulturkampf: anyone committed to replacing an "institution by another institution—better and different" ends up "being absorbed by the dominant structure" (230–32) in the process. The perennially contested Shakespeare phrased this dilemma more concretely in the sonnet that speaks, like Gold, for the industrial worker whose "nature becomes subdued to what it works, like the dyer's hand."

# 3 Red Letters/Dead Letters

You aint done nothin' if you aint been called a Red.
—folk song

Bartleby had been a subordinate clerk in the Dead
Letter Office at Washington, from which he had been
suddenly removed by a change in the administration.
—Herman Melville, "Bartleby the Scrivener"

Despite the success of *Jews Without Money*
with the reading public and despite its lasting stature as representative proletarian fiction,
Gold's work met considerable resistance on the
left. Melvin Levy, himself a proletarian novelist
(*The Last Pioneers*) and party member, reviewed
Gold's book in *The New Republic* and pronounced it "a failure when judged by the standards of proletarian literature." Levy's judgment shows how Gold was habitually at odds
with the "ultraserious" Communist party establishment (Herbst 43; Langer 115). Nevertheless
he answered Levy diplomatically in a letter to
the editor. "I submit myself to these standards;
indeed I have fought for their recognition for
more than ten years" ("Proletarian Novel"). Various manifestos, published throughout the
twenties and thirties, support Gold's claim.
Published in 1921, "Toward Proletarian Art"
gave the very phrase "proletarian literature" its

"American currency" and ended the middle-class monopoly on literary radicalism (*Anthology* 162; Folsom, "Education" 243). The most striking evidence of Gold's effort to graft the prevailing literary ethic, naturalism, onto his proletarian aesthetic appears in his correspondence during the 1920s with Theodore Dreiser. As Kenneth Payne demonstrates, these letters show Gold's commitment, ultimately realized in *Jews Without Money*, "to illuminate and demystify 'the imperial forces' of Dreiser's early naturalism, to unmask them as the . . . consequences of American capitalism, itself neither mysterious nor unassailable" (28).

Right after publishing *Jews Without Money*, Gold codified this revisionist naturalism as "proletarian realism" in a *New Masses* editorial (*Anthology* 206). On the strength of these credentials, Gold incorporated his reply to Levy's critique into his ongoing brief for proletarian art. Here, however, Gold discriminated among the arts to stress the difficulty of achieving proletarian realism. Implying that a proletarian aesthetic in literature will be harder to establish than in other arts—and obliquely echoing the call in "Proletarian Realism" for a "cinema in words" (207)—Gold's reply to Levy names only two models for emulation, the filmmaker Sergei Eisenstein and the painter Diego Rivera. Characteristically setting a standard by invoking a canon, Gold launched into an inclusive, antinomian exhortation:

There is nothing finished or dogmatic in proletarian thought and literature. We cannot afford it. We are pioneers moving through a hostile and virgin forest. It would be fatal for us to have fixed minds. Proletarian literature is taking many forms. There is not a standard model which all writers must imitate or even a standard set of thoughts. There are no precedents.

The allusion to winning the American west and the adjectival pair "hostile and virgin" echoes the frontier evocations in Gold's first manifesto as editor of the *New Masses*, published in 1929 and entitled "Go Left, Young Writers!" Thereafter, such frontiersman posturing became a rhetorical habit (*HM* 34). Gold's letter to the editor also betrays an intention contrary to his overt insistence on openness and diversity insofar as this posture signals an imperious will to conquer "thought and literature" (and perhaps complicates Gold's references in *Jews Without Money* to such dubious heroes as Buffalo Bill and Teddy Roosevelt).

Within five years of this plea, much was "finished" and "fixed" in proletarian writing. No sooner had the literary left reached a consensus in support of Gold's agenda when the Communist party discarded "proletarian realism" to replace it with the expedient catholicity, the ostensibly more inclusive cultural standards of the Popular Front. But by this time, with inspiring "energy and confidence and crudeness" Gold's "proletarian realism" had made its mark throughout American writing beyond the intentions of the party (Aaron 230; Arnowitz 235; Nelson 164). As Gold boasted, "overnight, almost like Byron, the concept of 'proletarian literature' became famous" and "important enough for Thomas Lamont's *Saturday Review of Literature* to 'demolish' it week after week" ("Notes" 2). Decisively institutionalized, "a proletarian tradition" had secured a prominent place "in American literature" by the middle of the decade, just as V. F. Calverton had prophesied in 1932 (Calverton 467; cf. Gold, *HM* 44–45; Rideout 237; Klein, "Roots" 135–36; Rahv 7–8; Kazin, *Starting* 12). "The vogue flared. The magazines of the Left carefully encouraged each newly converted apprentice, whether he had any craftsmanship or not. . . . Not all Marxist criticism was applause for neophytes. Such serious critics as Hicks, Gold, Freeman, and [John] Strachey tried to set up standards for a Marxist analysis of literature" (Strauss 363–64).

Like most established movements, proponents of proletarian literature and of the Popular Front movement that absorbed literary proletarianism held conferences—a series of writers' congresses between 1935 and 1941—and, under a party-sponsored imprint, International Publishers, issued an anthology entitled *Proletarian Literature in the United States* in the year of the first congress (Kempton 131–32).

Today the most revealing contribution to this "pioneering" anthology, which Gold helped edit and contributed to, remains the introduction by Joseph Freeman (Sussman 177). Here Freeman assayed a detailed, reasoned apologia for the overt revolutionary partisanship that the volume sponsors. Freeman's essay complements Gold's heated, elliptical earlier manifestos. In Irving Howe's and Lewis Coser's tendentious view, "Freeman wrote with surface reasonableness that set him apart from" his comrades, particularly "veteran hacks like Gold" and made Freeman "a far more effective spokesman for the party line" (277). Reminiscences that evoke Gold flicking ashes on the rug or spitting in the street reinforce this suggestive, if overstated, stylistic distinction (Robinson 124; Freeman, *AT* 257, 568).

Such differences notwithstanding, Freeman praised Gold as a Kulturkampf warrior for the "fight" Gold put up in *Jews Without Money*, a fight for "his right to describe in fiction the life of the tenements" and for the proletariat as a whole, "for the expression of his own experiences in art" ("Introduction" 18). A year later Freeman elaborated his view of Gold as "a protagonist of revolutionary literature" and praised "his irritable polemics against aesthetes who supported the status quo" (*AT* 633). Freeman identified "the secret of his passionate literary style" with "his poverty" and his rare resistance to the opportunism rampant on the literary left. Freeman claimed Gold—"older" (by five years) and "more experienced"—as a mentor who "corrected my dark thoughts" (323). According to Arthur Casciato, Gold and Freeman worked as "close allies," despite consequential differences, in promoting proletarian culture (20).

Though Freeman made a sophisticated, erudite case for proletarian literature, his rhetoric, like Gold's, insists on Kulturkampf. Accordingly, he opened his anthology introduction by rehearsing the party-line view of art as "a political weapon" in "the future social war . . . the class struggle . . . the battle" ("Proletarian" 9). All these martial phrases appear on the very first page and thus establish an urgent sense of embattledness.

This essay, though, offers more than a battle cry. It also articulates arguments for literary Marxism that resonate today, despite a self-congratulatory academic tendency to dismiss the more popular, more influential Marxism of the thirties as "vulgar" and theoretically benighted (Concha xix; Said 160–61). Writing expressly as a Marxist, Freeman tackled "literary theories"—the title of a *New Masses* book review—as early as 1929. Scooping both Randall Jarrell and Geoffrey Hartman, Freeman noted how criticism was overtaking "creative literature as a result of cultural disruption and social division" (12). Freeman followed this diagnosis with a metacritical anatomy of literary theory since Kant. Largely a critique of what today's theorists recognize as discursive "privileging" on the part of bourgeois opponents as well as his fellow Marxists, Freeman's review endorses the argument for literary Marxism that the book under review, *Literature in the Light of Historic Materialism*, by Mark Ickowicz, makes. "Ickowicz quite correctly repudiates the legend that Marxists believe that the economic factor is the only factor important in the development of art. Quite the contrary, Marx, Engels, Lenin, and other historical materialists have always pointed out that the political forms the class struggle takes, legal codes, religion, philosophies, morals, etc., have influenced social life" (13). Conceding that "in the case of art the economic factor is the last instance," Freeman insisted that "intermediate factors such as 'mythology' play a more direct role."

Obviously Freeman resisted "vulgar Marxism." In fact, he could never overcome the aesthete's sensibility that he formed as a Columbia undergraduate during the teens and as an aspiring Greenwich Village bohemian in the twenties (Beck 102–6). Freeman's first wife, Ione Robinson, reports that when they met in 1929 in Mexico, where she was studying with Rivera and where Freeman was serving as Tass correspondent, he courted her by reading Proust aloud:

It is really very difficult being in love with a Communist. And yet he is very sweet. The other day he asked me if I had ever read Marcel Proust, and when I told him I didn't know who Proust was, next time he brought along a volume called Swann's Way, which he read aloud over the bowl of chilies. The only trouble is that there's always such a commotion being made by the generals drinking tequila at the bar and shouting Viva this and Viva that, that I scarcely know where we are in the book. (104)

And after marriage, back in New York: "Every morning at breakfast, Joe still reads Proust. It seems that the character called Swann is like one of the movie serials I used to go see every Friday night. He never ends. What he says and does bores me. But if I do not listen to Joe reading about Mr. Swann at breakfast, he claims that I am unable to understand what real genius is" (123).

For all Freeman's mealtime Proust-mongering, he was, Robinson recounts, quick to denounce as irresponsibly apolitical a still life of flowers that she painted.

When Joe came home and saw my flowers, he got angry. He sat down and gave me a long lecture about art belonging to the people and that I should paint workers in "compositions with content." . . . I felt I had committed a crime. He gave me the New Masses and told me to look at the illustrations. The only thing that I seem to see in the drawings there is that everyone is being hit over the head, hung, or starved. . . . I am certain a worker would like to look at a beautiful flower more than at a picture of a policeman hitting him over the head. (127)

Less than a decade after Freeman lectured his wife, contradictorily, with Proust and agitprop, and helped introduce Americans to Marxist literary theory, he had been, as he put it, "excommunicated" from the Communist party ("Finland" 2) and "fired from the left" ("Forbidden" 2). Though "completely detached from all organized groups" (122), Freeman continued to insist that "Lenin's writing is a thousand times more creative than Proust's" ("Mask" 12). Despite such pronouncements, the *Partisan Review* essay in which this one appears, "Mask, Image, Truth," offers a forceful defense of literary Marxism against a hegemony-based disparity among critics: "When a Marxist critic describes facts as he sees them, he is a paid propagandist for the Kremlin. When a bourgeois writer utters the meanest, most malicious, most barbarous superstitions, he is exercising his right of free speech, his 'intellectual integrity' and his imagined monopoly on truth" (3). After thus indicating the burden of literary Marxism, Freeman tasked the Marxist critic with disciplined iconoclasm: "He rips the masks off the priests of art . . . exposes the propagandist, translates the equivocal images of verse into the lucid conceptions of prose, holds the author responsible for his characters when they actually do speak for him" (8; cf. *AT* 338).

As an example of such "irresponsible" mystification or privileging, Freeman cited Thomas Wolfe's *Of Time and the River* and challenged prevailing formalisms that implicitly condoned Wolfe's bigotry. An idealizing sequestration of "creative" writing had become a pretext for the most vulgar bigotry. "The word 'creative' is beginning to reek with the grease of piety" ("Mask" 3). This piety, according to Freeman, enabled Wolfe to regard *Kike* as "a 'poetic' adjective" (4). Moreover, the obscurantism underlying this piety separates "images" and readers' "consciousness" of "the whole culture" that produces images (17). Thanks to such attitudes, writers like Wolfe, and the readers he appeals to, can claim to "transcend" political and moral accountability by framing bigotry as fiction: "Now if the author had written such stuff directly in an article, he would have been damned by everybody from the *New Masses* to the *New York Times* and placed in the same category with Hitler, Goebbels" (5).

Throughout this essay and through much of Freeman's criticism during the decade, such hyperbolic name-calling punctuates his more tempered, analytic observations. Thus Freeman took care to distinguish Wolfe's Goebbels-like "caricature" of Abraham Jones from Shakespeare's and Joyce's more complex "character-drawing" in rendering Shylock and Bloom. Freeman argued that Marxist criticism, discerning and socially responsible criticism, had to be concerned with rhetorical effects and the genealogy of images (6–7).

Without the Communist, the propertied classes would *unrestricted* bamboozle the masses with their 'democratic' images. Without the Marxist critic the 'faustian' creative writer would *unhampered* propagate his poisonous ideas in obscure, false but effective images.

*These images are effective because they have* three thousand years of religion, three centuries of bourgeois ideology, the whole culture of capitalism to sustain them; because they evoke emotional habits, deep, deep in the souls of most of us. (8–9)

For Freeman the left Kulturkampf of the thirties became a contest over what criticism is for and, by the time he published this essay, he realized that his struggle was almost as much with the left establishment as it was with the still more powerful literary mainstream and its persisting tendency to "mistake the circumscribed experience of the middle class for the whole of life," when "bourgeois life seems eternal, natural, alone real" (16). During the thirties Freeman's work was increasingly marked by this tension: his lifelong Marxist resistance to covert bourgeois thought-control—hegemony—as well as the cruder bigotry it produced met his growing disaffection from the then marketable pieties of left dissent. This tension may account for Freeman's oblique effort to rescue Marxist criticism from the orthodoxy that frames "Mask, Image, Truth." Freeman opened this essay by comparing the homegrown "pogrom on Marxian criticism" with "the same situation . . . in the Soviet Union" (3) and closed by addressing "sincere . . . fears" of "procrustean communist formula" (15).

Freeman avoided codifying a privileged "realism," a designation he distrusted "because it depends on the illusions it seeks to destroy" and so avoided privileging any particular school of "realism"—social, socialist, proletarian, or otherwise ("Realism" 2–4). He resisted settling definitively on what might be "alone real," unlike both his "bourgeois" antagonists and more orthodox leftists, in-

cluding Gold and other proponents of proletarian literature. For Freeman theory became resistance to dogma, not
its production. He shared this understanding with his second wife, the painter and art critic Charmion von Wiegand. Together they made the passage from Communism
to antinomian socialism and back to the more aesthetic bo-
hemianism of his youth. She accounted for the failure of
"social realism" by recounting the failure of her own paintings, industrial landscapes, to meet with approval from
Soviet culture police in the early thirties:

The Russians didn't like them at all because they said there were
no people in them. You've got to show people doing things . . .
they saw things only through theory. They never saw things with
their eyes. And since they were going to change the world they
wanted to impinge these theories on your work. . . . You can
make cartoons or clichés but you can't make art where it's inte-
grated with the landscape and the people. (Von Wiegand 15, 89).

Even at the height of his own complicity with such Socialist Realism, Freeman seemed so uneasy with it that,
enlisting Eisenstein as his expert witness, he managed to
package easily ridiculed "tractor art" as a "deliberate parody on the Hollywood Wild West movie," a successful effort to produce "a new social content" out of an "old form"
(*AT* 594). More abstractly, Freeman faced the same problem
in his introduction to *Proletarian Literature in the United
States*, where he insisted that "art varies with experience,"
so that proletarian writing can "sustain Marx's theory"
without providing "an illustration" or even any acknowl-
edgment of it (15–16).

Unfortunately, the Communist party and its more orthodox adherents—Mike Gold, for example—prevailed
over Freeman's antinomian Marxism, his antidoctrinal
proletarian aesthetic. This contest made for a long-
troubled erratic passage for Freeman. From partisan advocate to unsponsored Marxist theorist, from propagandist to fiction writer, Freeman took many confusing, tor-
menting turns before his expulsion from the party in 1939.
The strain becomes most apparent in the contrast between

nuance and the respect for history that marks "Mask, Image, Truth" and the bland evasiveness of "Toward the Forties," Freeman's 1937 introduction to *The Writer in a Changing World*, a collection of papers delivered to the Second American Writers' Congress. Here Freeman veiled his growing knowledge of the Moscow purge trials with a quote from George Brandes—"The question of party . . . is not a question of judging the past but of shaping the future"—only to devote much of the essay to a revisionist, congratulatory Popular Front history of American literature as "above everything else a literature of protest and rebellion" (13, 20). Losing Stalin's atrocities in a cursory survey of current events—a catalogue of ubiquitous, cataclysmic, political violence (15)—Freeman celebrated the recent institutional establishment of literary leftism—especially at the First American Writers' Congress in 1935—as the dawn of a "new creative period" (27–33; cf. Beck 111–12).

In much current opinion, thanks to Frank Lentricchia's *Criticism and Social Change*, Freeman's lasting significance seems to rest narrowly and unfairly on his role at this First Writers' Congress as a foil for Kenneth Burke, the "repository of principles" for "healthy criticism" (19). Lentricchia recalls Burke's address to the congress, "Revolutionary Symbolism in America," which challenged the "party line" that both Freeman—"throbbing like a locomotive"—and Gold—"the steamroller"—hastened to defend (Cowley, *Dream* 278). Limiting himself to a partial account of the incident, Lentricchia overlooks the pronounced ambivalence in Freeman's labeling Burke "a traitor" (*Criticism* 22). Malcolm Cowley's first-hand account, from which Lentricchia draws, recalls Freeman amiably apologizing to Burke. Arthur Casciato elaborates on Cowley's recollection, arguing that "most of what Freeman said" in rebutting Burke "seems mild, even conciliatory," and contrasting Freeman's warmth toward Burke with that of other more threatened ideologues (61, 64). Daniel Aaron's detailed history singles out Freeman as Burke's only intellectual equal at the congress: "Freeman alone seemed to catch the drift of Burke's remarks" (*Writers* 308). Burke's own report on the congress, for the *Nation*, praised "the vitality and organizational ability of the Communist party" and the Kulturkampf consensus it generated, "the general feeling that all these writers must somehow enlist themselves in a cultural struggle . . . with relation to historic necessities . . . a concept of social responsibility, of *citizenship*."

Like Burke's, Freeman's thirties experience—his work as a critic and promoter, his role at the first two American writers' congresses, even the intellectual content of his two marriages—anticipates and illuminates the now familiar, diversely construed conflict between intrinsic and extrinsic critical approaches, formalism and historicism, aesthetic "disinterestedness" and partisan engagement. Freeman began grappling with these conflicting claims at a time when literati, on both sides of these divides, were near unanimous in assuming that such divisions were clear-cut. Now many of us think we know "better." Cowley remembered Freeman as trying "to serve as a mediator between the two" (*Dream* 144). Like many literary Marxists today, Freeman was troubled and sustained by this tension between aestheticism and social consciousness.

This tension tended to keep Freeman from the intellectual crudity, the supposedly vulgar Marxism, that marks so much of Gold's work. Just as he resisted party line simplifications while a Communist, he abjured the popular "god that failed" posture after he left the party. In a letter of 1939, written but never sent to Mike Gold, who stayed with the party, Freeman ridiculed as "stereotyped calumny" rumors that he was working on a book "which will repudiate the Communist Party" (Hoover, Box 152). Though his first novel, *Never Call Retreat*, verges on such a repudiation, Freeman's primary antagonism, to fascism, dominates the book. In August of 1945, he wrote an assessment in *Life* of postwar U.S.-Soviet relations, endorsing a continued alliance. Freeman never ceased considering himself a socialist, as a lecture Freeman gave at Smith in 1958, a rare public performance, illustrates. Freeman reminded his audience that not everything Communist, not even everything Russian, was tainted by Stalin during the thirties:

Despite the horrors of the Age of Assassins, the Thirties were also progressive in other parts of the world—in Russia, for example. While Stalin was shooting his rivals wholesale, Russia succeeded in building a type of economy which the world had never seen before. This economy has raised Russia to second place in the world and many people in this country are now afraid it may raise her to first place. It . . . has made Russia strong, given her the lead so far in the conquest of space. ("Vision")

(It's easy now to scoff at such claims, but Freeman spoke when many believed Soviet Communism to be, according to Daniel Moynihan, "at its apogee, its progress declared irreversible"; hence this regard for Soviet achievement wasn't some marginal or outré view but a national consensus exploited by right and left alike, which determined the 1960 U.S. presidential election.) Maintaining his dialectical historicism, Freeman identifies the McCarthyite "attack on the Thirties" as the complement and product of Stalinism—"the Terror of the Fifties" that "ruined . . . many innocent lives."

Freeman's historical orientation remained Marxist in precisely the sense that Lentricchia endorses: "Marxism as a kind of rhetoric, a reading of the past and present, invites us to shape a certain future" (*Criticism* 12). "Refusing to adopt the posture of either the 'penitent sinner' or the 'groveling informer,' " Freeman insisted that, when subpoenaed, he declined "to testify against his friends and former political comrades; he would only say he entered the communist movement as a poet in 1922 and departed as a poet in 1939," after which he "recorded his own disillusionment . . . in a private manner" (Lowenfish 11, 13). Clearly Freeman fits none of the procrustean assumptions reserved for "ex-Communists." This may explain why Freeman never achieved the renown—or notoriety—of either Gold the party stalwart (whose *Jews Without Money* remains in print as a paperback and has recently made it into a major anthology), or of the more vociferous, dogmatic ex-Communists who became well-paid apologists for the status quo.

A few years before Freeman's death at sixty-seven in 1965, Daniel Aaron documented Freeman's importance in helping build a literary left. Aaron also singled him out for particular attention as the only American ex-Communist who could assess the Communist experience "with the philosophic insight of a Silone, a Koestler, or a Malraux" (377). Twenty years later Edward Said observed that the heritage of left criticism in this country might owe as much to Freeman as it does to Randolph Bourne and Edmund Wilson (161). Even derogatory accounts of Freeman's influence indicate his importance in building and maintaining a cultural left during the late twenties and early thirties; hence Kenneth Lynn's sarcastic citation of Freeman as America's Communist "authority" on literature (*Airliner* 93) or Max Eastman's unforgiving remembrance of Freeman as the Machiavellian "priest" and hypocritical "inquisitor" of literary Communism (*Artists* 124, 141, 148). The perception of Freeman's influence on the left was such that, according to Malcolm Cowley, around 1933 "one prominent stockbroker gave a luncheon for Joe Freeman and Mike Gold" (*Dream*, 155). The broker's explanation: "Comes the revolution and he wants to have friends on both sides of the barricades." Freeman's prominence in the mid-thirties even brought him a fleeting moment of media celebrity at the hands of America's most notorious gossip columnist, Walter Winchell; typically sophomoric, Winchell dubbed Freeman "the Reditor of the New Masses" (Lowenfish 10).

For all this recognition of Freeman's importance, "the Communist party's most talented intellectual" remains a footnote (McConnell 179; Starobin 253; Beck 101). As early as 1933, Granville Hicks speculated as to the conditions that had prevented Freeman "from winning the reputation to which he is entitled" (*Tradition* 296). This devaluing of Freeman may be due to the kind of influence he exerted and the kind of conflicts he represented. According to Jo-

seph Starobin, Freeman had an especially tonic influence
as a founding editor of the *New Masses* from 1926 to 1934
and was responsible for whatever intellectual vitality the
magazine managed to achieve in its early years (32). Freeman's influence extended beyond the *New Masses* and the
Communist cultural apparatus. James Wechsler recalled
not only Freeman's appeal and influence, but how much
he embodied the conflict inherent in honorably practicing
literary Communism:

One day while walking around Greenwich Village headed for nowhere, I met Joe Freeman, then the editor of the *New Masses;* I
knew him slightly and liked him. A Columbia graduate of an
earlier radical generation, he was a gay, lively man who did not
wear a communist leer or speak the language of pious certitude;
I had even heard rumors that he was intermittently accused of
nonconformity. . . . What I did not guess was that at exactly that
time he had asked to be released from his post at the *New Masses*
[after] having served long and faithfully. (125–26)

Freeman's influence as writer on the left peaked just as
his influence as an editor and cultural arbiter started to
diminish, upon the publication of *An American Testament* in
1936. This autobiographical account of becoming a Communist, a conversion narrative, "made a great impression
on the youth of the thirties, and was one of the few American radical memoirs to echo abroad, where Victor Gol-
lancz's Left Book Club reprinted it" for British readers (Starobin 253). One *New Masses* staffer who worked with Freeman recalls "that young men read his book in England
joined the party in hordes" and remembers him as a "charismatic speaker" who could make "every single person" in
a large audience feel "that he alone was getting Joe's attention." Though this reminiscence may overstate Freeman's
influence, it corresponds with the Eugene Lyons's Red-
baiting assertion that Freeman's account of Communism
"was making converts among" American youth "long after
Mr. Freeman himself would have repudiated" it (113).

Whatever his personal charm and however diverse and
productive Freeman's career—as a Village bohemian, as a

cultural commissar, as a muckraker and foreign correspondent, as a radio and screenwriter, as a publicist—*American Testament* stands as the centerpiece of this long and varied life and as a central text in the history of American literary leftism. As counterpoint to the conversion represented in *American Testament*, Freeman spent the next thirty years—the rest of his life—writing his autobiography, mostly in fictional form, as a counterconversion narrative. Though most apparent in the novels Freeman published in the forties, this effort also marks the shorter publications and unpublished, unfinished material of the fifties and sixties.

In his 1958 lecture at Smith, Freeman looked back on the thirties with critical nostalgia, invoking Wordsworth and Yeats to account for his own revolutionary fervor. Without much novelty but with an unequivocal rhetorical design, Freeman went to each poet's best known postrevolutionary musing, book 10 of *The Prelude* and "Easter 1916." Both these poems voice a generational "excitement of the *promise*, the vision of the good life, the better world" and an impatience "for . . . redemption and liberation" as well as disillusionment at the suffering such desire caused. Both poets speak in the first-person plural in the well-known passages Freeman cited, indicating an effort to speak representatively. Such an effort distinguished Freeman's work from the outset. Consider how Freeman subtitled *An American Testament: A Narrative of Rebels and Romantics*. As Freeman began to compose this narrative in 1934, he wrote to Lewis Mumford and asked to see any of his correspondence over the past twenty years "that might give the atmosphere of the time." Freeman described his autobiography-in-progress as "a study of the leftwing literary movement" and of "the growth of our leftwing literary movement as a whole." He singled out Mike Gold's "subsequent development" as an especially "interesting" instance of the literary Communist bildung.

As he shared the burden of building a literary left with Gold, Freeman also did his most memorable writing as an autobiographer. *American Testament*, which recounts how he came to Communism from his native shtetl in the

Ukraine, resembles *Jews Without Money* in that it evokes a conversion, a crucial transformation in the narrator's consciousness, and proposes its narrator's conversion as exemplary. Although it has lapsed into obscurity (and is out-of-print), Freeman's narrative has been extolled by Max Eastman—notwithstanding his mockery of Freeman in 1934 as the "pure but diplomatic priest of Stalinism"—as "the best and most engaging book written by an American Communist" (*Artists* 124; *Love* 604). "A really swell job" was Gold's judgement in a letter to Freeman (Hoover, Box 152).

Freeman's reconstruction of his Jewish immigrant boyhood in New York and his intellectual coming-of-age ranks with *Jews Without Money* as "one of the few classics of the proletarian movement in American literature" (Guttmann 139). Where Gold's story simply recounts the making of a revolutionary, *American Testament* details the making of a revolutionary intellectual and the encompassing historical transition from "the medieval village" to "the metropolis of America," the encompassing historical pattern with which Freeman identified himself (15–16). According to Daniel Aaron, it also enacts painfully and unconvincingly the never-ending struggle between poetry and politics (149–50). Hence Freeman concerned himself with chronicling and understanding a generational movement as much as with recounting his own self-fashioning in the ongoing unfinished autobiography that he only began in this narrative and continued to write for the rest of his life, each installment "only a prelude to transformation" (*AT* 17).

Oddly, the historical resonance of *An American Testament* depends on the psychological and rhetorical dissonances that it fails to resolve (cf. Aaron 151–56). Freeman described this dissonance between the party and bohemia right in the middle of *American Testament* (292). This central chapter closes with Freeman expressly associating a generational tendency with his own vocational crisis, which would prove to be lifelong:

For my generation the problem of art and revolution was to re-main a thorny one . . . [a] struggle with the most elementary questions. This struggle led me to literary criticism, which I have always liked to read and never liked to write. Now there was no longer a choice. When you are deeply rooted in one world, you can create poems and stories out of emotion, out of unquestioned presupposition. When you are in the No Man's Land between two worlds, you must analyze, weigh, compare, question, test, hypothesize. The quest of the intellect transforms the assump-tion of the emotions . . . gives you an opportunity for grappling with fundamentals. (320)

Freeman structured his narrative so that the most pro-nounced, prolonged instance of such "grappling" in *Amer-ican Testament* covers, in six chapters, his Soviet sojourn in 1926 and 1927.

But if I had been animated only by the Communist viewpoint, there would be nothing to tell here in this story, which is not about Russia but about the education of one man. . . . In Mos-cow I realized once more how deeply rooted I was in the bour-geois world. Alongside of Communist thought and belief, there existed in me the various illusions I had absorbed in the schools, the streets, the books of capitalist civilization. It was one thing to believe in an idea abstractly, quite another to come up against it in the flesh. Reality had a way of shaking dreams and reviving prejudices: logically you may justify war; in the trenches you will perhaps throw down your gun and run in terror. (504)

The rhetoric of these two passages reveals the self-division that Freeman confided to Daniel Aaron some twenty years later. Freeman never made "flesh" the ab-stract Marxist ideas that *American Testament* affirms (156). Thus Freeman recalls how he came to work at the *Masses* hoping "to reconcile . . . warring" commitments to "Pal-grave . . . Beauty" and "Marx . . . Justice" (53). In this "in-ward struggle between his literary loyalties and the claims of the 'selfless, incorruptible' party" nearly all the literary characteristics of *American Testament* favor traditional, nineteenth-century literary practice. Such practices pre-suppose—or privilege—"the bourgeois illusion" of individualism (Lentricchia, *Ariel* 23). As Thomas Doherty argues, the very choice of the autobiographical form by any "Marxist ideologue" constitutes a paradox: insofar as autobiography cannot rest on "the imperatives of Marxist historicism . . . an ideology that denies historical uniqueness . . . , the autobiographical act itself borders on ideological heresy" (105). Freeman's own realization that autobiography should function as "only a historical footnote" confirms this principle (*AT* 595). Less troubled by such contradictions, Freeman's comrades at the Second American Writers' Congress voted Freeman's autobiography the best American "biography" of the year.

Repeatedly resorting to bourgeois individualism, Freeman's rhetoric in *American Testament* compounds the heresy and contradictions. The two passages quoted above contain, for example, generational and hence collective metaphors—images of trenches and No Man's Land still fresh from the Great War that shaped the consciousness and literature of Freeman's generation, the so-called Lost Generation. But if, as Paul Fussell has demonstrated in *The Great War and Modern Memory,* the physical conditions of the war (which Freeman—like Faulkner and Fitzgerald—knew only as a stateside soldier but not as combatant) radically altered perceptual and discursive assumptions, Freeman's narrative never incorporates these changes, although the will to do so—the "quest" to "transform"—pervades the book. The understanding of "dialectical materialism" that Freeman cultivated in the Soviet Union, in pursuit of "Eisenstein's Holy Grail," signals this will to inhabit a space not "of ready-made *things,* but a complex of *processes*" (597). As a writer, though, Freeman never achieved this liberating fluency. His conventionally academic resort to chapter epigraphs, for example, appeals to established and canonic voices—such cultural commodities as Joyce, Gorky, Shelley, Hart Crane, even Nicholas Murray Butler.* Freeman thus implicitly endorsed prece-

---

* Butler (1862–1947) served as president of Columbia University from 1901 to 1945, dramatically transforming the university during his tenure. He was also the Republican vice-presidential candidate in 1912.

dence and prominence as the ground of discursive authority. Likewise, Freeman became most vehement in denouncing the Zhadanovist "eagerness to dynamite the past" and in affirming the Trotskyist view of gradual cultural change, the necessity of working with inherited cultural material, and the consequent understanding that revolutionary culture should incorporate the bourgeois canon:

All knowledge and all insight to which men had attained everywhere at any time was essential. In the revolutionary pantheon we retained Plato as well as Engels, Shelley as well as Mayakovsky, Spinoza as well as Lenin. In the wasteland of theft and blood which the bourgeoisie was leaving behind it, socialism alone could preserve the cultural heritage of the past. (637)

Freeman's facile expropriation of Eliot's influential "wasteland" critique reinforces Freeman's broader brief for the "pantheon" as promoted by Matthew Arnold, whose discursive dominance colored Freeman's work as much as it did Eliot's (Eliot 129). Freeman also sounds like Matthew Arnold in repeatedly lamenting his displacement "between two worlds" (McConnell 98–100).

An even more obvious precursor with respect to Freeman's high culture man-of-letters persona is Henry Adams, his image of himself "floundering between worlds passed and worlds coming" (*Education* 83). The publication of Adams's *Education*, coinciding with the Great War generation's coming-of-age, had a marked impact on its consciousness (Klein, *Foreigners* 15; Hicks, *Tradition* 134–39). As early as 1923, Freeman began to argue, in "A Note on Henry Adams," that Adams's *Education* leads obliquely but inevitably to an embrace of Marxism.

Consequently, Freeman strained to misread Adams into the left canon that he promoted throughout the thirties:

I was interested in how people became socialists; the transition from the old culture to the new was bound to be the universal spiritual change of our times . . . a period of profound social transmutation. In his day St. Augustine had explained how a Roman gentleman had become a Christian. Dante's "New Life" was the testament of man caught between the Middle Ages and the Renaissance. Rousseau bared his heart to the world at the moment when bourgeois society was preparing to overwhelm and exterminate feudalism. And in our country, Henry Adams, moving from an agrarian culture to a machine age, had summed up his long education by saying that he should have been a Marxist. (*AT* 619)

Freeman's emphasis on Adams as a model of (even incomplete) Marxist self-fashioning reveals how much more *An American Testament* works as a de-conversion narrative than as a persuasive account of conversion, as Freeman claimed. The Marxist passage in Adams's *Education* that Freeman alludes to hardly "sums up" the education; it appears early in a chapter concerning the narrator's discovery of evolution in his late twenties. After introducing Marx as a vexing pedagogue he would "sooner or later . . . have to deal with" (72), Adams restricted his understanding of Marxism to methodology and heuristics, paying no attention to the passion for justice that drew Freeman and Gold to Marx. "By rights, he should have been also a Marxist, but some narrow trait of the New England nature seemed to blight socialism, and he tried in vain to make himself a convert. He did the next best thing; he became a Comtetist" (225).

Freeman's fusing Adams and Augustine into a single legacy, moreover, obscures their incompatibility, which Adams (as his own pseudonymous "editor") announced in his preface. Adams contrasted the articulation of orthodoxy or "unity" that Augustine's *Confessions* achieves and the heterodox "multiplicity," the disciplined skepticism, to which Adams educated himself and his readers: "The habit of doubt; of distrusting his own judgment and of totally rejecting the judgment of the world; the tendency to regard every question as open" (6). Yvor Winters's blunt complaint that "Adams did not care for truth" (399), echoing as it does Adams's own insistence that "convenience was truth" (457), underscores the incongruity in Freeman's adopting the *Education* as a model. Freeman's syncretic legacy needs to be read against Adams's confession to William

James that his interest in Augustine lay entirely in the bishop's finesse in mastering the narrative form of belief, solely in the "romance" of belief (Scheyer 36).

Thus the twentieth-century autobiography with which Freeman expressly affiliates his own testament is decidedly incompatible with Freeman's overt partisan agenda. Adams rejected conversion, denied the possibility of knowing any certain transcendent truth, and scoffed at all current doctrines of progress. As Kenneth Lynn puts it, "Adams was haunted by the thought that all his formulations of human experience were wrong," and thus in *The Education* "unsparingly reviewed all the occasions on which he had failed to grasp the meaning of events" ("Adams"). Freeman would not reach this Adams-like capacity for self-criticism for another decade—after his expulsion from the party, which had stigmatized "intellectual doubt" (Hook 89). Hence *American Testament* closes with Freeman's return from the Soviet Union in 1927 as a confirmed convert, "with new eyes" and with his "internal struggle allayed" (667).

Life in the Communist movement appeared to be something more simple, more normal, more meaningful than I had realized earlier under the spell of certain middle-class assumptions. . . . You no longer sought a way of life. The Communist movement had given that to you as to millions of others . . . a world-wide movement whose aims and requirements transcended those of any individual . . . an inspiring national force in American life.

Freeman added a coda to this prophetic avowal, a letter to Hedda—his German comrade and confidante—that suggests a lag between his certain conversion to Communism and the integration of that certainty into his literary vocation, as "a writer" groping "to the new literature which speaks for the new world" (668). Freeman's vocational uneasiness here recalls Edmund Wilson's caution, in "Marxism and Literature," as to the contradiction that dogs literary Marxism. Wilson distinguished Dante's vision, which Freeman had appropriated along with Adams's and Augustine's, from "the Marxist vision," and

identified the latter as a program "of actual social engineering": "Society itself" becomes "the work of art." Wilson added: "In practicing and prizing literature, we must
not be unaware of the first efforts of the human spirit to
transcend literature itself" (*Triple* 289).

Both Freeman's and Gold's autobiographical conversion
narratives illustrate, however, that "literature" is never
"transcended," only displaced in their autobiographical
narratives by oratorical closure.* Freeman paused to reflect
on this dilemma: "I was thinking how good it would be if
language could stir people as music did. Shakespeare did
it, and Shelley. But this was an arid time. There were so
many harsh, important things to say that you could not
stop to model melodies around the imperative idea" (646).

Despite Freeman's resignation here from "literature" as
high art, his narrative—more than Gold's—includes much
of the "literary" sort of writing he wistfully renounced.
Such writing is most pronounced where Freeman restages
his family life (25–26, 261, 411) and in his chapter-long
portrait of a Maude Gonne-like "bad Communist" named
Gretta (397) and her Lady Gregory-like opposite, Hedda
(529–35). This writing prompted one reviewer to praise
Freeman's "keen and quizzical eyes," his "gusto and creative energy," and to "hope Mr. Freeman has in him the
architectural gift to compose novels as well as poems"
(*BRD* 1936). On the strength of such "literary" merit alone,
*An American Testament* belongs with Malcolm Cowley's
much better known, "creamier" and intellectually less ambitious memoir, *Exile's Return* (Howe, "Critic's"). Marcus
Klein finds in Freeman's "literary communism" the convergence of bohemian modernism and Depression realism
as well as the continuity of the Lost Generation aesthetic
("Roots" 139). As a chronicle, too, *An American Testament*
matches and may surpass Cowley's account. Thus Horace
Gregory's praised Freeman's book primarily as "literary
history" (*BRD* 1936).

---

* Familiar, now suspect Romantic definitions of literature govern this
conclusion, as in Yeats's elevation of honest "poetry" above manipulative
"rhetoric."

One obvious reason for the passage of *An American Testament* to oblivion may lie in its failure as a conversion narrative and, more demonstrably, in its unwitting persuasiveness as an anticonversion narrative. The most favorable reviews dwelt on both the fullness and the dividedness of *An American Testament*. Louis Kronenberger, reviewing it for the *Nation*, found "a bulging narrative of ideas and personalities." It "rolls out and over, and against, such a devouring tide" that it leaves "the author himself . . . helpless." Hence Kronenberger praised Freeman for his "experiencing nature" and for his "ardor without fanaticism." Malcolm Cowley at the *New Republic*, then probably the most Olympian voice on the literary left, hedged his praise of Freeman's verve and of his narrative as "a poet's book" with sobering speculation:

The whole idea of revealing one's reasons for living is a poet's idea; the thorough politician takes them for granted. But Freeman, in writing about his own motives, has to labor under a self-imposed political censorship. He cannot reveal incidents that are too damaging to his own party, and neither, in this personal record, can he too deeply offend its enemies. . . . He has to choose his words like President Roosevelt speaking in Governor Landon's home state. In spite of this limitation, he makes you feel that he has written a completely honest book.

Cowley added later that Freeman's "account is as honest as he could make it while following the party line" (*And* 106).

Soon after publication in 1936, the censorship of *An American Testament* went far beyond the self-censorship Cowley detected (McConnell 112–16). According to Daniel Aaron, these favorable reviews and the literary marketplace in the mid-thirties made *An American Testament* "a potential best seller" (384). It sold, however, only four thousand copies. The Communist party condemned the book for its treating Trotsky ambivalently rather than vilifying him according to the party line, and for failing to idealize Stalin sufficiently (Lowenfish 11; cf. Freeman, *AT* 632, 626). Yielding to party demands, Freeman halted distribution of his book and stopped trying to promote it. Aaron recounts that Freeman forbade advertising and the very mention of it in the pages of *New Masses*.

The effacement of *An American Testament* was compounded in the fifties by McCarthyism (Lowenfish 12). Without mentioning his own contributions, Freeman broadly reconstructed the conditions that obscured his achievement by recalling the thirties as "a period of *trauma* . . . an emotional block" ("Vision"). Writing in 1958, he accounted psychologically for this "war on the intellectuals, on the vision of the thirties":

As in every terror, the victims are themselves affected by this falsification. People who are penalized for their ideas are not inclined to remember. . . . We know what memory is like when painful. We all tend to forget—or, as the Freudians say, repress—painful memories. And so many people have written falsely about the Thirties in books, newspapers and magazines and have spoken falsely about it on the witness stand, all in good faith. . . . There is that little thing called *survival*. It is a crime to have shared in the vision of the Thirties, then you are asked to write about it. O yes you *did* share that vision! but it is dangerous to admit it now. So you write: WHO—ME? The story is *now* that we knew all along that Communism was fraud. Communists were all stupid, inefficient, cruel, crazy for power, corrupt foreign agents. We never really believed that insane, bloodthirsty ideology . . . we were always at heart patriotic . . . and, anyway, we are fighting those sons-of-bitches today and we hope that our former friends and comrades *do* lose their jobs and go to jail.

The intellectual McCarthyism that has obscured *An American Testament* may still be in force today. It takes the form, ironically, of academic Marxism. Out of a fear of seeming "vulgar," such Marxists evade "the problem of Stalin" and, out of an anxiety not to appear influenced by such naive base-superstructure paleo-Marxism, produce instead an "elitist deformation of Marxism" (Dowling 12; Concha xix). This persisting and deforming consensus may help account for the continued inattention to *An American Testament*.

Considered from the standpoint of its divided rhetoric

and the censorships that have obscured it, *An American Testament* brings the romance of Communist conversion and the promise of a proletarian aesthetic, such as *Jews Without Money* enacted and articulated, up against the limits of literary Marxism. In his next book, a novel entitled *Never Call Retreat* and published in 1943, Freeman looked back on the lessons learned in reaching these limits, lessons based in part on the brief unhappy shelf life of *An American Testament*. This emphasis on lessons led the reviewer for the *New Yorker* to judge Freeman's novel "thoroughly educational" (*BRD* 1943). Josephine Herbst observed this pedagogic motive in the narrator's "passion for sharing what he knows." Another reviewer, Diana Trilling, described the subject of these lessons as "one of the greatest available to the modern novelist—the relation of the individual to the forces of history." Four years after his expulsion from the Communist party, Freeman preserved, elaborated, and probed—with the distance that fiction allows—the Marxist understanding of history that he had spent the past twenty years cultivating.

From the perspective of independent postparty leftism, *Never Call Retreat* quite literally frames history just as Lentricchia proposes framing it, as "a conversation . . . whose discourse is rhetorical and without foundation and whose ends are never assured because rhetorical process, unlike teleological process, is free" (*Criticism* 13; cf. Rideout 270). Insisting on such conversational freedom, Freeman frames the narrative as a psychoanalyst's transcript of his sessions with Paul Schuman, a Viennese refugee and history professor newly arrived in New York just before Pearl Harbor. A secondary conversation, within the psychoanalytic frame, revolves around narrator Schuman's scholarly interest in an early Christian scholar-martyr, Saint Eusebius, whose defense against heresy charges and exchanges with his captors Schuman/Freeman imaginarily reconstructs in the later concentration camp flashback sections of the novel.

Finding it "more than a novel" and even "too rhetorical," reviewers insisted that Freeman's book be read as a "treatise" and a "thought-provoking argument" (*BDR* 1943). The harshest review came from Mark Schorer. Apparently trapped in his own narratologic formalism, he complained that *Never Call Retreat* "reads like an *endless* editorial" (emphasis added). More dialectically, Diana Trilling ascribed the book's faults—the "woodenness" of the protagonist, the excess length, "its heavy burden of erudition"—to its "serious, scholarly, ambitious" agenda, which earned it a "special place." Another reviewer suggested that "its faults as much as its virtues" make it "large and impressive."

The book's strains are even evident in Freeman's resonant title. As the title page epigraph reminds readers, the title echoes the third verse of Julia Ward Howe's "The Battle Hymn of the Republic," an apocalyptic call to arms. Steinbeck's more obvious and better known titular allusion to "the grapes of wrath" in Howe's song reflects the tendency of thirties literary leftism to draw heavily on abolitionism for its usable past, particularly striking in the title of Gold's 1936 play about John Brown, "Battle Hymn." This habit of adapting abolitionism and the Civil War as a secular radical tradition took its most memorable form in the name of the American contingent that fought for the Spanish Republic, the Abraham Lincoln Battalion (Klein, *Foreigners* 89).

The Spanish Civil War is central to *Never Call Retreat*. Paul Schuman's first wife, an English Communist who introduces him to Shelley, is killed in an air raid while doing war relief work in Spain. Near the end of the novel, his courtship of his second wife includes a visit to see *Guernica* soon after its arrival in New York. Consequently the contemporary resonance of the title probably inflects its more perennial, more native familiarity. The tension that results from the narrator's movement between the familiar and the unprecedented—between Julia Ward Howe and Picasso—unsettles this entire novel, since the particular phrase of Howe's that Freeman chose insists on the inconclusiveness of such apparently apocalyptic struggles as the American and the Spanish civil wars. *Never* here precludes the apocalyptic frisson, the promise of resolution and the catharsis of rage, that Steinbeck exploited in his borrowed title.

Max Eastman focused on the title phrase in trying to explain what troubled him about Freeman's novel: "In a novel entitled *Never Call Retreat*, Joe seems to have tried, by brooding over various historic parallels, to make his mum retirement from a position of loud influence understandable. The title was inspiring, but I could not find the meaning of the book" (*Love* 605).

As Eastman suspected, the books' meaning does reside, morally as well structurally, in its title. Freeman's apparent allusion to Marx's classic of revolutionary frustration, "The Eighteenth of Brumaire of Louis Bonaparte," shows how ambitiously Freeman envisioned his novel as a critique of his own lapsed party Communism and an effort to talk himself and his readers into a renewed antinomian revolutionary fervor. Playing "the great expectations of the century" (*NCR* 710) against what ensued—the censoring of *An American Testament*, Stalin's purge trials, the Comintern's treachery against Spanish anarchists, and the Molotov-Ribbentrop pact—Freeman elaborated on the "hangover" that, according to Marx, follows early revolutionary hopes.

The social revolution of the nineteenth century cannot draw its poetry from the past but only from the future. It cannot make a start on itself until it has stripped away all superstitions concerning the past. Earlier revolutions needed the recollections of world history to render them insensible of their own significance. . . . Then the rhetoric transcended the substance; now the substance transcends the rhetoric. . . . Bourgeois revolutions, like those of the eighteenth century, sweep on rapidly from success to success . . . men and things seem set in sparkling diamonds, ecstasy is the spirit of everyday; but they are shortlived, soon reaching their climax, and a long hangover afflicts society until it learns soberly to assimilate the results of it periods of storm and stress. Proletarian revolutions, on the other hand, . . . constantly criticize themselves, continually interrupt their own progress, return to what seemed completed in order to start all over again . . . till a situation is created from which retreat seems impossible. (Marx 289–91)

Marx's imperatives—to question, criticize, and un-mask—inform Freeman's novel just as they inform what Marx calls the poetry of revolution. As a poetics of revo-lution, *Never Call Retreat* responds to the lesson Marx urged—to "learn soberly to assimilate . . . storm and stress." Hence the narrator's fascination with the French Revolution, subject of his dissertation and first book as a professional historian, recalls Marx's preoccupations in "The Eighteenth of Brumaire" with the legacy of Bonapar-tism and the dialectical undoing of revolutions (*NCR* ix, 102, 256, 544–60). With his narrator's shifting, antiapoca-lyptic rhetorical position, Freeman addressed the heuristic problem Marx identified in distinguishing rhetoric from substance. Substance, for Freeman, both in and out of the party, involved the fusion of sentiment and realpolitik into socialist morality, the development of which *An American Testament* articulated. Freeman cited Gorky in summing up this morality: "Oppression makes people cruel" (*AT* 641).

In *Never Call Retreat*, the narrator's martyred father, a theater critic turned professional revolutionary, with "all the answers . . . for whom the past was to be tran-scended," acts on Gorky's insight (130, 150). He also comes to embody it and the commitments it engenders, suc-cinctly articulated in the counter-salutation with which he and his comrades displace the increasingly popular greet-ing of *"Heil Hitler"*: *"Freundschaft und Freheit."* "It was the hail and farewell of Viennese socialists" (129).

The fact is my father had begun calling himself a socialist. I doubt whether he belonged to any political party. . . . His views on the evils of the old order and the marvels of the new were abstract and, for the most part, I suspect, a tribute to prevailing literary fashion. But my father was an eloquent man; when he de-nounced the evils of "child labor, imperialist exploitation, pov-erty, inequality, and war," my young heart trembled with name-less fear and hatred of the prevailing world. On the other hand, his glowing pictures of the future classless society filled me with a wonderful sense of hope and longing, though if anyone had asked me what it was I longed for, I would have had a hard time explaining. (25)

The father's martyrdom results from the attack, in 1934, by Austria's Dolfuss government on a communal worker's housing project where Schuman's father lived and worked (231–33). This narrative fact serves as an oblique criticism of the American Communist movement, which fomented dissension on the American left, sabotaging united protests against the massacre (Hook 110–11; Klehr 112–14). Even if his actions and assumptions can no longer be identified with Soviet socialism, the socialist heroism that the narrator identifies with his father sustains the heroic ideal that Freeman first discovered in the Soviet Union during the twenties, during the sojourn that *An American Testament* elaborates. The writers Freeman met there "resembled such literary heroes of my boyhood as Sir Philip Sidney and Dante in combining action with poetry" (*AT* 574).

*Never Call Retreat* turns on the narrator's efforts to reconcile his father's socialist morality with his own historian's skepticism. At the beginning and near the end of this circularly plotted novel, in the passages set in New York, this tension proves paralyzing. Freeman at once qualifies and deepens the appeal of the father's socialist eloquence with the narrator's remembrance of the family's Czech peasant housemaid, a devout Hussite, whose life stories "lent poignant meaning to father's theories," without diminishing the traditionalist authority that her eloquence rests on, Bible-reading and anti-ecclesiastic dissent (26). Combined with his scholarly interest in the French Revolution, which parallels Freeman's own (Hoover, Box 91; McConnell 129–30, 48), the narrator's formative emotional connection with the Reformation recalls Gramsci's praise of the synthesizing force of Marxism: "It crowns the whole movement for intellectual and moral reform. . . . It corresponds to the nexus between the Protestant Reformation plus the French Revolution" (87).

Reinforcing this affiliation, Freeman invoked Milton throughout the novel. While passages from Milton's poetry and prose head several chapters, the story itself includes a volume of Milton's poems that Schuman's first wife leaves behind as a postmortem "refuge" (688) and an essay on Milton—our antifacist "contemporary"—that Schuman works on in New York (696). In an unpublished poem from the twenties, Freeman echoed Wordsworth, asserting, "Milton, America needs thee in this hour" (McConnell 99). In *An American Testament* he enrolled Milton in his revisionist pantheon of artist-propagandists along with Aristophanes, Juvenal, Jack London, and Upton Sinclair (370). In 1940, Freeman wrote an essay on Milton, much like Paul Schuman's, entitled "A Champion of Freedom," and applied for a Guggenheim Fellowship to complete "a modern . . . popular biography of Milton," of which he composed a substantial draft despite his failure to win the fellowship (Hoover, Box 122). At Freeman's death two of his most substantial uncompleted projects echo Milton's tutelary example: a novel entitled *The Forbidden Tree* and an autobiography entitled *Paradise Forever* (McConnell 151, 171, 174).

The most resounding appeal to Milton in *Never Call Retreat* recalls the recent party-led effacement of *An American Testament*. In a discussion of *Areopagitica* between Schuman and his poet friend Kurt Hertzfeld—foremost among the novel's several model characters—Kurt defends the party decision to censor his own book (*NCR* 192–94). Here Freeman has the narrator read Milton's celebration of books "as lively, and as vigorously productive, as those fabulous dragon's teeth [that] may spring up armed men."

The scholarly narrator's doubts, in contrast to his father's and his friend's faith in party ecclesiasts, are conditioned throughout the narrative by academic historical research as well as by first-hand experience: his World War I ordeal; his contacts with Vienna's aristocratic haut monde and bohemian demimonde; his participation in the struggle against fascism between the wars; and, especially, his concentration camp captivity. These camp passages center on Schuman's friend Kurt. As a camp inmate in Schuman's company, this "belated Shelley of the Rhine-land" (201) undergoes a transfiguring metamorphosis (450, 503): a boyish bohemian poet who disciplines himself into a self-effacing ideologue, Kurt ultimately offers himself as a scapegoat for his fellow inmates, erstwhile comrades who had made him a pariah for his gracious dissidence. As rhetorically dependent on polarities in this book as he was in *An American Testament*, Freeman counterpointed Kurt's martyred generosity with the Machiavellian savvy of his party boss Hans Bayer. Freeman's narrator takes pains to show that Kurt learns Hans's lesson, though he refuses fatally to apply it: "Misfortune had salted his lyricism with satire," so that "the face of Shelley" took on "the glint of Heine" (438).

Like several characters in the novel, Kurt serves mostly as a site of rhetorical contestation and an occasion for moral reflection. As a shortcut around fuller characterization, Freeman takes rhetorical advantage of the literary left's hagiographic enlistment of Austrian and German martyrs to socialism during the thirties (Casciato 51–52, 227; Gold *CW* 230). Like Schuman's father and the three women—French, English, and American—that Schuman loves, Kurt is an idealized projection of the narrator's moral and intellectual desiderata, a lesson bearer. As such, Kurt recalls similar but less complex accounts in *An American Testament* of the revolutionary artists and ideologues that Freeman knew in the twenties. As a charming Shelley figure, Kurt recalls a less chastened German literary Communist whom Freeman met in Moscow, also named Kurt. He "was known throughout the world . . . as a clever theoretician, orator, writer, and organizer. . . . Kurt's style was like that chapter in *Ulysses* in which a baby's birth is described in all styles of English literature from *Beowulf* to our own day" (*AT* 515). Like the fictional Kurt in his novel, the historical Kurt endangered himself with his rare combination of talent and honesty: "At first it seemed to me there was no sting in Kurt's satire, but later I wondered whether a man in so responsible a position was not playing with fire, whether a mind could not become so agile that at the most critical moment it might slip out of its own grasp" (515). This Kurt is also disciplined by his party boss, with a personal letter from Stalin.

The end of *Never Call Retreat* reinforces Kurt Hertzfeld's role as moral cynosure insofar as Freeman expressly reincarnates him in American guise as Michael Gordon (715, 739). An aide to Schuman's only American friend, a publishing magnate he studied with at the Sorbonne in the twenties, Gordon, is a twenty-something California poet-athlete who put himself through Harvard before enlisting in the Lincoln Battalion to fight Spanish fascists (665–79). While Kurt endured ostracization and battering from his comrades and torture and execution from his Nazi captors, Gordon is Red-baited out of publishing and OWI work— by a southern senator who speaks of "Jew York"—and into infantry combat (707, 672). Thus this American beau ideal gets to complete Kurt's unfinished business, the defeat of Fascism. Freeman's schematic ending is compounded by the narrator's marriage to Michael Gordon's almost saintly sister Joan, a Columbia librarian. This relationship cures him of the depression that prompted him in the first place to seek out the psychiatrist whose transcripts constitute the entire novel.

These intellectual and poetic alter egos and revolutionary beau ideals bear a prophetic reproach. Repeated invocations of Jeremiah in the last third of the novel reinforce this concern. The aptness of Jeremiah for this concentration camp section of the novel not only rests allusively on Jeremiah's distinction as "the prophet . . . shut up in the court of the prison" (Jeremiah 32:2); Jeremiah's voice also recalls the tenacious jeremiad strain in American writing that Sacvan Bercovitch has limned. The authority of Jeremiah as a particularly American prophet was grafted onto the proletarian literary agenda during the Popular Front period of the mid-thirties; thus Alfred Kreymborg's pithy Petrarchan sonnet entitled "American Jeremiad" appeared in *Proletarian Literature in the United States*, the anthology that Freeman introduced and Gold helped edit (Gold, *HM*

40). This strain apparently became a commonplace on the literary left, as Gold's identification in 1937 of himself and his associates as "hairy Jeremiahs" suggests ("Notes" 2).

Freeman associated all the jeremiadic echoes in *Never Call Retreat* with Kurt's betrayal by his party mentor, Hans (McConnell 131, 29). Thus Freeman frames their climactic confrontation with echoes of Jeremiah cursing: "And ye shall be an execration, and an astonishment, and a curse, and a reproach; and ye shall see this place no more" (42:18). In the first echo, a chapter epigraph, God not only curses but, in the unquoted lines preceding the epigraph, also threatens the saving remnant with the same "fury . . . poured forth upon the inhabitants of Jerusalem" (499). Then Schuman recalls how Kurt, newly wise, confronted his treacherous comrades with Jeremiah's most resonant question: "Why do the wicked prosper?" (507). The sequence of Kurt's commentary on this confrontation, "Three cheers for Micah and three more for Jeremiah," hints at the passing of the naive populism that much intellectual leftism, particularly the Popular Front of the thirties, rested on (518). Micah, the lowborn prophet of the peasantry, yields to the harsher, more urbane, more worldly-wise and world-weary captive, Jeremiah. In thus identifying Kurt with complex and authoritative prophecy, *Never Call Retreat* aims its prophetic critique dialectically at the left Machiavellianism that, as much as self-serving "bourgeois" myopia, produced and sustained totalitarianism in the thirties.

With the old-fashioned eloquence and prophetic authority that marks Kurt's apostasy and martyrdom, Freeman strives to disintegrate what Mike Gold had achieved in *Jews Without Money* thirteen years earlier—the fusion of American Communism and Old Testament prophecy. But Freeman's effort, to disable rhetorically and so discredit the belief that had enthralled him over two decades, failed. The contrast between the rhetorical effect that Freeman ambitiously struggled for and the "wordy and uncontrolled" novel (Cowley, *And* 110) that he produced becomes plain in the narrator's description of *Guernica*. A newly arrived refugee from fascism, like Schuman himself, Picasso's painting promises the peaceful apocalypse that Freeman, failing to achieve it himself in his long Communist affiliation, provided his narrating alter ego. After reminding him of his wife's "grave in Andalusia," *Guernica* overcomes Schuman with intimations of redemption: "Soon the drawings transcended all personal grief and said things even beyond Europe and America united at this moment by Picasso's art. The irresistible power of the painter shattered stereotypes of jaded vision, ripped old veils asunder and revealed mankind in the new light of struggle, suffering, hope and redemption" (685).

For Schuman, the painting contains "the ever-changing sum total of human history" in which

everything appears simultaneously; all sides of object and event are here as past, present, and future merge into a vast sun of time to illuminate man's august drama hitherto seen through a glass darkly, now face to face in the fiery hour when indignation and despair are engulfed by a love which rises gigantic with the sword of righteousness in its hand.

In a protracted phantasmagoric dream, Freeman offered a prose analogue for *Guernica* (as Schuman had read it): "A terrifying serial of mad scenes" and "images surging in swift disorder" in which widely separated moments in history, often in the form of Dos Passoesque headlines— Dante, Danton, Christ, Caesar, Schopenhauer, Adams, dynamos—converge with the promise of transfiguring "the fear of death" into "ecstasy" (544–49, 560). Freeman's praise of Eisenstein also resonates here. In 1930, Freeman described the Soviet director as a formalist "who gets his effects by eccentric parody and the 'pathos of heroism' " and who, "though he will reproduce historic scenes with accuracy . . . will not hesitate to introduce a puppet of Napoleon Bonaparte as a commentary on Kerensky" (*Voices* 264). Freeman's emphasis here suggests how much both Eisenstein's and Picasso's works serve as nonverbal analogues for the dialectical deformation that Freeman pursues in these passages.

Most striking in Schuman's description of *Guernica* are his clumsy echoes of Saint Paul (the narrator's namesake). Incongruously, Schuman echoes Saint Paul's world-loathing promises of transcendence in response to a painting that offers an unprecedented, defiantly earthy protest against transcendence. According to John Berger, *Guernica* "abstracts pain and fear from history and returns them to protesting nature" (169). In Berger's argument, the painting "illuminates" nothing beyond bodily pain: "All the great prosecuting paintings of the past have appealed to a higher judge—either divine or human. Picasso appeals to nothing more elevated than our instinct for survival."

Freeman's eager appropriation of Picasso here in *Never Call Retreat* rests on an even more outrageous misreading than his appropriation of Adams in *An American Testament*. Hence Freeman's narrator converts the disillusionist that Berger describes into a necromancer: "Picasso waves his necromantic brush and now you see how man is, man in the making, eternally organic and spiritual, the ever-changing sum total of human history" (*NCR* 685). Although occasions for yoking Pablo Picasso and Henry Adams are rare, Joseph Freeman's fascinating if unwieldy narratives offer such an occasion. That Freeman, a theoretically sophisticated and highly cultured litterateur by all conventional standards, could misread these works so egregiously indicates some virulent repression or deep-seated evasion in the operation of his consciousness and sensibility.

What *Guernica* and Adams's *Education* share is their evocation of disillusionment and articulation of fatalism in the face of the violence that impels both historical change and natural continuities. Such educating disillusionment links Freeman and his narrating alter ego Schuman. Yet the framing of *Never Call Retreat* reveals how intent Freeman was on repressing this education. Nowhere is this more evident than in the prefatory note to the novel. Entitled "The Aim is Victory," its optimistic jingoism desperately, even hysterically, celebrates and exhorts "the marvelous courage and fighting stamina of a fresh free people" pos-

sessed of "everything . . . required for victory." In con-
junction with the new age—an American Century—that
the novel's ending greets, such blatant propaganda belies
both the historian's skepticism that informed Paul Schuman's antifascist commitments and Freeman's own scru-
pling, as a Communist critic during the thirties, to avoid
the crudities of agitprop and self-flattering appeals to "realism." Contrary to widespread stereotypes, Freeman's
postparty liberalism was much more "vulgar" than the
Marxism that he practiced and preached as a party member, much of which stayed with him after his party years.
This residual rigor accounts for the pedagogic virtue that
reviewers ascribed to *Never Call Retreat*.

Whatever its failures and fissures, Freeman's novel was
troubling enough to some influential readers to provoke
new efforts to repress his work. Though less public, these
efforts resembled the Communist campaign against *An
American Testament* seven years earlier. As Joseph Starobin
recounts, "the book was scheduled to be made into a war-
time motion picture when the project was scotched—according to Freeman's account, by Howard Fast and left
wingers on the West Coast, who refused to give a 'renegade' his chance in Hollywood" (256).

Freeman's only other published novel, *The Long Pursuit*
(1947), indicates that, unlike the more protracted and presumably more traumatic disillusioning ordeal of his break
with the party, this defeat by the American image industry
markedly altered his sensibility, his style, and his politics.
More a petulant sketch than a novel, *The Long Pursuit* recalls nothing so much as the movies of the late forties and
fifties that savaged the same coastal media that produced
them, and which by this time employed Freeman, who
wrote for radio and for the legendary publicist, Edward
Bernays. This cinema subgenre includes: *The Bad and the
Beautiful, All About Eve, The Sweet Smell of Success, A Face in
the Crowd,* and *The Great Man.* The similarity is reflected in
Freeman's plans to write a another media novel—about
publishing—as a companion to *The Long Pursuit.* Tenta-

tively titling it "The Brass Ring," Freeman wanted it to read "like a Preston Sturges movie" (Hoover, Box 122).

Drawn from Freeman's work for the "Information Please" radio show, *The Long Pursuit* recounts in third-person narration the USO-like tour of military bases in Europe by a similar show, "Five Star Chat." "Culture with a brass band, genius and jive, a minstrel show with good conversation . . . Aristotle with Glenn Miller . . . it educated millions . . . brought philosophy, history, science and literature to the villages and cities of the land" (83–84, 110). The novel's main character, Emory Flush, the program's MC, started "Five Star Chat" as a movie theater feature and in the process became a Hollywood power broker "from [whom] you can go anywhere," a "bully" who makes associates "want to puke" (86–87, 176–77). The novel functions as a single-minded indictment and exposé of Flush's power—to the point of equating it with the European totalitarianisms that preoccupied Freeman. Thus the novel's foremost Freeman surrogate, an urbane writer named Mark Bingham and the brains behind "Five Star Chat," upsets Flush merely by pontificating about world history:

The twentieth century . . . has seen the biggest free for all fight for power in a thousand years. We like to think powerful men are superior men. They are—in power. If the men who govern the world hadn't been mad with fear, ambition and self-adulation, none of this would have happened. Now the monster which their stupidity evoked is crushed. But their ambition will grow, their fear take on more and more fantastic proportions, their self-adulation will have no bounds; and, crazed with power, they will rush us blindly into new catastrophes. (101; McConnell 163–64)

Much later, Freeman's omniscient narrator reinforces this fatalism, this resistance to optimistic illusion. In a long passage, punctuated by appeals to Hobbes, Byron, Schopenhauer, Socrates, and Bingham's own beloved "minister grandfather," Freeman's narrator has Bingham recount how he lost his "real self" to amoral history (239–41). Freeman barely masked the autobiographical strain governing this meditation and, in a single sentence turnaround, finally—characteristically—relinquished the hard-earned skepticism, the ideological negative capability, that he had sustained throughout the novel: "The problem of power seemed perennial and insoluble. This forced him to recover his faith in ideas. He now told himself that the material conquest of the earth could only lead to universal destruction if it was not based on true ideas, on those first principles that transcend and persist through time" (241).

Freeman followed this willed resolution with a facile deus ex machina happy ending, in which the tyrant Flush conveniently dies in a car crash, freeing his underlings for lives of "hope" (the last word in the book). As Jonathan Arac observes, this conflict between a rigorous, unsettling examination of power and a willful, universalizing rhetoric of hope, between demystifying analysis and remystifying theology, is a chronic pitfall of left discourse (270).

Reviews of *The Long Pursuit*, much harsher than reviews of Freeman's first novel, accounted variously for the book's failure of negative capability. A "very, very serious" attempt to write caricature, to satirize "preposterously unbelievable" characters, it bored and disgusted at least two influential reviewers (*BRD* 1947). A more sympathetic reviewer, Herman Wouk, responded to Freeman's autobiographical subtext by remarking that, despite his "acute observer's eye and powers of analysis," the novel's style "is one of the casualties of the revolution." This undigested revolutionary residue diminished Freeman's second and last novel, in striking contrast to the sweepingly Mann-ish *Never Call Retreat*. Thus the reviewer for the *New York Times* judged *The Long Pursuit* "a lively and mildly amusing novel of what happens to nice people when they work for the wages of Hollywood" and complained that it "tries too hard too entertain."

The last two reviews suggest Freeman's continuing value with respect to at least two intellectual challenges that remain at the center of literary politics today. Hermann Broch recognized the novel's political depth when, in a letter to Freeman, Broch praised the work as "a book of indignation . . . a necessary complement to *Never Call Retreat*—the satyr play after the great tragedy" and as a "social document" that "sharply portrayed" conditions in postwar Europe (Hoover, Box 171). As a discerning critic of power, Freeman characteristically falters at the close of his narratives, when he apparently pulls back from acknowledging the troubling discoveries that the narrative enacts. This disjunction marks both his fiction and *An American Testament*.

A story that appeared in *Harper's* in 1941 seems an exception to this refusal to confront the implications of the discoveries that his narratives realize. Entitled "God Sees the Truth," it echoes and mordantly revises Tolstoy's "God Sees the Truth but Waits." Freeman set out frankly to "butcher a masterpiece" (543). Freeman's conversational narrators are an American and a German, both loyalist veterans of the Spanish Civil War, who meet in a Greenwich Village public library. Between them, they transform Tolstoy's tale of hard-earned redemption, of justice delayed but ultimately achieved, into a thersitic discovery of the prevailing politics whereby "when a crime is completely successful . . . it ceases to be a crime and becomes a virtue" (548). In the wake of this discovery, the German refugee who has seized the narrative alters Tolstoy's heartening title to fit an era in which "not the murderer but the murdered man is guilty": "God Sees the Truth But Won't Talk." This transcendent muteness was as close as Freeman came to inhabiting the impasse his narratives repeatedly reach and to confronting the possibility of knowledge without salvation. Such a confrontation would have involved deferring endlessly any gratification of the desire for action-enabling moral clarification that informed all his work.

Freeman's narratives and his critical essays invariably articulate this desire—for justice and for the nonviolent maintenance of an equitable social contract. For Freeman, this desire colored all reading and writing; thus pausing in the library, the primary narrator of "God Sees the Truth" realizes:

You don't really escape. You read a story about Peru or Madagascar and the characters become your sisters and your cousins and your aunts, your friend who was killed in Spain, or the front-page names who were great statesmen and are going to be shot tomorrow. Afterward, you go home, think about the characters, change the plot and try and figure out the meaning of the story. (542)

Freeman's work also probed the inevitable complicity, the righteous guilt of the culture producers—makers of "front-page names" as well as monumental novelists like Tolstoy, Viennese history professors as well as Hollywood scriptwriters—whose professional practice, manipulating words and ideas, contradicts their commitments to justice, equality, and reason. Freeman attributes such complicity with unjust power, which artists and intellectuals traditionally purport to scorn, to bohemian writers and party apparatchiks in *An American Testament;* to academics and professional revolutionaries in *Never Call Retreat;* to entertainers and journalists in *The Long Pursuit.* For all his understanding of this dilemma, Freeman's failure lay in his refusal or inability either to find a frame of acceptance for this complicity as inevitable or to show himself and his readers a means of overcoming it.

# 4 The Nineteenth of Brumaire

He had studied Karl Marx and his doctrines of history with profound attention, yet he could not apply them.
> —Henry Adams, *The Education of Henry Adams*

This machine kills fascists.
> —placard on Woody Guthrie's acoustic guitar

We don't know how to use our modernism.
> —Marshall Berman, *All That Is Solid Melts Into Air*

Freeman's and Gold's careers and commitments diverged sharply in the last two decades of their lives, when Freeman became a moderate socialist and a public relations executive and Gold, sticking with the Communist party long after it had lost its credibility in most Western eyes, worked as an obscure party newspaper columnist. Like the differences between their approaches to literary Marxism during the twenties and thirties, this later divergence need not obscure the common lifelong concerns that overrode their partisan affiliations and disaffiliations. Most notable among these concerns is their persistent effort to address questions raised by modernity—the consciousness altering material changes that occurred so rapidly during the past two centuries—and modernism—the artistic counterresponse to these changes. Coinciding with Gold's and Freeman's formative years, these changes radically altered artistic expression and representation in their lifetimes (Singal 7–8). But, as Marx passionately argued in "The Eighteenth of Brumaire" and elsewhere, radical change seldom brings revolutionary transformation and often tends, ironically, to reinforce the status quo.

Freeman's later, largely unpublished work vividly reflects these questions and their persistence. He kept redrafting and retitling an autobiographical narrative, usually cast as a novel, while producing numerous sonnets and unproduced screenplays (McConnell 169–75). These last two literary practices seem at odds with each other. This tension—between a form of archaic, self-consciously artificial Elizabethan craftsmanship and one that belongs distinctly to twentieth-century technology and mass culture—is, as Daniel Bell argues, characteristically modern and modernist: it pits the museum against the machine (Bell 122–25).

These divided aspirations run throughout Freeman's telling, mostly unpublished poetic efforts, which mix traditional poetic diction and canonic allusion with the ephemera of commercial mass media:

Milton, America needs thee in this hour
Thy organ could bellow through the phone
"Wheat is one-sixty, there's a drop in flour—
President spends his afternoons alone."    (McConnell 99)

The heavy perfume of the pines
Fills all the valley (COOLIDGE DINES
WITH PARTY LEADERS) gray and still
the west grows dark (NEW SENATE BILL.    (100)

Similarly, Freeman counterpoised "the canon" (Yeats and Joyce), in the following, against more accessible cultural commodities (comic books, sensationalist best-selling novels that have "gone Hollywood"):

Get wise! Forget the high and tender muses;
To hell with Shem and Shaun; the cant of song

All covered with embroideries by Whosis
Will ruin you good; you know that art is long;
Write Superman and Counterspy, they pay;
Or do Forever Amber. . . ." ". . . What are they?"

Freeman's career in radio, television, and public relations and the stack of unproduced movie and broadcast
scripts, about Americans liberating Europe and about the
pursuit of money and celebrity, drafted during his last two
decades clash markedly with this evident antipathy to
modern mass-culture (Hoover, Boxes 120, 132, 134, 137–
40; McConnell 169).

This clash also reveals the sort of cultural impasse that
Freeman, as well as Gold, created and then confronted in
their efforts to reconcile left politics and modernist poetics,
a traditionally schooled literary sensibility and an egalitarian commitment to the masses. The enthusiastic prophecy
of the French moviemaker Abel Gance illustrates how such
aspirations as Freeman's, the will to synthesize individualist "great traditions" with modernity's mass movements,
pervaded modernism: "Shakespeare, Rembrandt, Beetho-
ven will all make films" (Benjamin 221–22).

Antonio Gramsci similarly rejected the more influential
dichotomy between traditional art and mass culture, a split
that reactionary modernists like Eliot and left modernists
associated with the Frankfurt School cultivated. Gramsci
argued that the compatibility envisioned by Gance, the
mutual enrichment "between popular and higher culture,"
results from the "flowering" of popular culture and the
"materialism" of revolting masses (87). In this century, according to Gramsci, Marxist intellectuals must foster this
conciliation.

Both Freeman and Gold pursued that convergence envisioned by Gramsci. Gold particularly was an early advocate of allying modernism and Marxism, a would-be
American Brecht (Bogardus 5–6; Dickstein, "Tenement"
64). An "anti-bourgeois" animus and a will to resist "commercial glitter and [its] false promise" (Bogardus) provide
the common ground of Marxism and modernism while a
shared "adversary habit" and resort to "military images"

produced similar rhetorics (Fussell, *Great* 106–7). Each discourse promised power as compensation for widespread perceptions of powerlessness. Consequently, modernists and Marxists alike were concerned to evoke this perceived powerlessness—the "fetters and limitations" that constitute these perceptions (Marx and Engels, "Ideology" 170, 175–77; Jameson, *Political* 19–20, 285–86; Robbins 235, 242, 244). Thus, in rescuing Flaubert from "the art-for-art-sakers, the esthetes of the social vacuum," Gold not only identified *L'Education Sentimentale* as "a bitter and mercilessly ironical . . . 'political' and 'revolutionary' novel," but also praised Flaubert's epistolary *nom de plume,* "Bourgeoisophobus" (*HM* 13).

Even more striking, the very title of the book in which Gold made this appropriation echoes, without any adaptation, one of the bitterest moments in the poetry of T. S. Eliot and in "high," or reactionary, modernism. The irony of Gold's allusion lies in his seizure of Eliot's title phrase—"The Hollow Men"—to title his own last book in 1941. Gold judged this poem an apocalyptic slander of the masses (*HM* 18). He quoted it to show "how foreign" what the poem expresses—what its producer and his "Harvard fascist" followers represent (*CW* 144)—was "to the feelings and lives of the American people." With a materialist reading of *The Waste Land*, particularly its "seven-page appendix of obscure and learned references," Gold set out to discredit Eliot's position as a modernist pioneer (20). Gold based this reading on Veblen's theory of leisure-class ostentation. From the same Veblenesque vantage point, Gold had, in an earlier essay, criticized Gertrude Stein as "a literary idiot" who "destroyed the common use of language" (CW 23–25). After conceding "evidence of wit and some wisdom" in Stein's "more popular writings," Gold situated her work "in the vacuum of a private income" where "you can write as you please." Even though Eliot earned his living, Gold nonetheless deemed *The Waste Land* "an exhibition of ostentatious waste and nostalgia for the antique" and thus turned Eliot's titular image of a "waste land" against Eliot and his legacy (*HM* 20).

When the narrator in *Jews Without Money* recalls seeing dozens of immigrant families "heaped like corpses" sleeping on a tenement roof and "mounds of pale stricken flesh tossing against an *unreal city,*" readers may hear line 60 of *The Waste Land* (126; emphasis added). In such passages, Gold availed himself of "the covert allusiveness of troping," the "modernist density" that "does not announce itself as literature" that Richard Poirier contrasts with the deliberately "difficult modernism" Eliot himself preeminently promoted (130, 101). Thus Gold allusively reproaches Eliot, whose aestheticized, mythically haunted cityscape masks material conditions, the immediacy and persistence of death and waste in modern cities.

Gold attacked the influential, "self-exiled, self-contemplating bourgeois" modernists and the "sterility of heart and mind in the works of the T. S. Eliots and Ernest Hemingways that should frighten a cautious conservative." Denouncing "Joycean intellectuals, hating life," Gold helped make such animadversions staples of Marxist criticism (*Reader* 164; "Notes" 2). Like Georg Lukács—a more sober and influential Marxist critic of literary modernism as reductive, distorting, and negating—Gold addresses the obscurantist technique more than the overt partisan positions of these writers (Lukács 45–46, 75–76; Arnowitz 235). Freeman moved from a similar premise to a less severe sentence in judging *Ulysses* "a great book [by] a genius" and "a marvelous mirror of the decay of capitalist civilization [which] raises the question [of] the future of the novel" (*AT* 636).

Freeman's more equivocal critique masks an embarrassing affiliation between literary Marxism and Eliotic or Joycean modernism, much as it exposes, as Freeman intended, "the gap between revolutionary politics and revolutionary literature," and much as it indicts the Veblenesque bases of much high modernism (*AT* 321). Thus Michael Folsom's praise for *Jews Without Money* as a superlatively self-effacing autobiography recalls the standard of impersonality that Eliot pronounced, in 1919, in "Tradition and the Individual Talent," by invidiously segregating the

man who suffers from the mind that creates ("Education"
246). Gold, however, could no more maintain this separa-
tion of man and mind than could Eliot (Poirier 103, 109).
Gold noted this tension in praising Jack Conroy's "semi-
autobiographic" focus in *The Disinherited* as a "virtue"
while castigating "the sickly introspection of bourgeois au-
tobiographers" (*CW* 216). Hence Gold's self-effacement,
his narrator's deference throughout *Jews Without Money* to
characters more daring ("Nigger"), more expressive (his
father), more suffering (Joey Cohen), wiser and kinder (his
mother) than himself, seems overshadowed by Gold's expressive subjectivity, the lyric aggressiveness of his yearn-
ing (Nelson 151; Klein, *Foreigners* 193).

According to Marcus Klein, Eliot and the other influential modernists associated with Eliot furnished Gold both
a needed enemy as well as "the basic tactics of his own
thought" ("Roots" 136–37; cf. Wald 14–15). Consequently,
"proletarian literature was a literary rebellion within a literary revolution to which it was loyal." Even in singling
out William Carlos Williams as a sympathetic model, a
proletarian's modernist "bigger than the Paris esthetes,"
Gold paid anxious homage to the aesthetes, hastening to
note that "in certain Parisian groups [Williams] ranks with
Gertrude Stein and James Joyce" ("What"). Klein's recognition that no ambitious American writer of the twenties
and thirties could entirely evade Eliotic modernism recalls
Freeman's view of Eliot as "a barrier that must be destroyed" (*AT* 240). Thus, Klein asks, "What, to put it
bluntly, did . . . Eliot, on his way . . . from Harvard to
Anglo-Catholicism, have to say to a young man named,
say, Irwin Granich?" ("Roots" 135). Klein lets Granich—
writing as always under the *nom de plume* Mike Gold—answer for himself. "Even at their best, in the supreme
expression of the bourgeois individualist, in a James Joyce
or a T. S. Eliot, defeat follows them like a mangy cur. They
are a historic blind alley and have no future. But year after
year I have seen the great proletarian dawn unfold over
the world, revealing new human miracles" (*Reader* 183).

Coming in 1953, the year of Stalin's death, and at the

nadir of McCarthyism, Gold's prophecy rings painfully false. Nevertheless, his diagnosis incisively anticipated a commonplace of late-century punditry—the paradox of modernism—its enabling failure, according Irving Howe, to negotiate a transit to material modernity: "Modernism can flourish only when it has it not triumphed" ("Thirties" 18).

The reaction to this impasse, as Neil Larsen argues, binds both literary modernism and Marxist agitation insofar as each seeks to penetrate the "opacity of the social" and to "rebel against the tyranny of the given" (xxxiii, 11). The result is an "aestheticizing of the [paradigmatically modern] crisis in representation and historical agency." Thus Freeman's dismissive description of the subjective, autobiographic mode common to twenties writing stands against his and Gold's adoption of this mode in writing their most memorable, conspicuously autobiographical books, *An American Testament* and *Jews Without Money* (Freeman, "Wilsonian Era" 130). This contradiction reveals how much they shared this modernist impasse with Eliot, Stein, and Anderson, among other major writers whom they disparaged, and how much, despite the illuminating Marxist explanations they counted on, the same "opacity" defeated them.

Gold's and Freeman's literary left Kulturkampf rests on as much as it resists the bohemian modernism associated with the twenties. Despite left attacks on the elitist aesthete strain of high modernism, Gold and Freeman, as literary Marxists, participated in this modernism, regarded either as a range of emerging formal and technical options or as the creed of impatience that resounds in Pound's order to "make it new" as much as in Marx's warning, in "The Eighteenth of Brumaire," that the revolution "cannot draw its poetry from the past, but only from the future" (290). In an early *New Masses* essay, Gold added a critical intensifier in an effort to expropriate this modernist conversation, urging in the title of his article: "Let It Be Really New!"

Notwithstanding the incongruities of practicing literary

Marxism under the aegis of Eliotic modernism, efforts on
Gold's part and on Freeman's to accommodate these discourses to each other rest on a view of Marxism itself as an
early form of modernism, a product of the same cycle of
revolution and reaction that Flaubert, Melville, Marx
worked from in the wake of the revolutions of 1848. Thus
the view of Marx as the "first and greatest of modernists"
and as a "kindred spirit of Eliot and . . . Stein" for which
Marshall Berman argues (129, 90) underlies Gold's and
Freeman's complex negotiations with literary modernism
and with prevailing assumptions about modernity. This
complexity, the extent to which Gold's and Freeman's literary Marxism shares the limitations and contradictions of
high modernism, further erodes received views of them as
crude, reductive, partisan, and sentimental.

Gold's and Freeman's observations and pronouncements on, their critiques of, and their engagements with
modernity, in two of its most conspicuous and conventional forms, movies and the architecture of cities, indicate
an overlap between literary Marxism and familiar expres-
sions of literary modernism, inasmuch as each strives to
contain the conflict between the progressive confidence to
"make it new" and an offsetting modernist hatred for modernity (Lentricchia, "Someone" 329). The resulting strategy of containment, which marks both Gold's and Freeman's work, produced the sort of left "Covert Pastoral"
that William Empson ascribed to "proletarian literature"
during its heyday, especially "common in present-day
[1935] Russian films" (6). While in the traditional pastoral
"simple people express strong feelings in learned and
fashionable language," Empson argued that in the covert
pastoral practiced by proletarian writers, tender indignation and observant alienation displace the traditional erudition, resulting in a comparable complexity and a comparable clash between the complexity and mobility of the
medium, on one side, and the didactic simplicity of the
message on the other (11–20).

Both Freeman and Gold assayed this distinctly modern
form of pastoral. Freeman transparently invoked the pas-

toral displacement Empson describes, the will to simplification that modern urban complexity provokes, in *Never Call Retreat*. Thus Freeman has narrator Paul Schuman sum up his Paris experience by recounting how the claims of sophisticated culture yielded to those of a higher and simpler, transcendent "human nature":

Before I had known Babette I was aware that the culture of the entire world could be found in Paris. But I imagined this culture was in the paintings of the artists, the books of the writers and the fine manners of the elite. Wandering through Paris on those Saturday afternoons with Babette, I learned that this culture was also in the streets and market places. Its essence was a freedom of the spirit, a tolerance of everything and everyone, a passion for experience of every kind. . . . Nothing was too trivial for our interest, too unworthy of our respect. (104)

In *Jews Without Money* the modern pastoral strain figures more consequentially. It becomes most pronounced in the chapter entitled "Mushrooms in Bronx Park." Here Gold established his narrator's alienated and thus, in Empson's terms, pastoral authority by threatening to belie, by deferring, the chapter's title. Gold's narrator spends ten pages detailing the suffering that summer in the city brings (141–51). Like Thoreau and Frederick Douglass and F. Scott Fitzgerald before him (and Bruce Springsteen after him), Gold intimates a didactic political critique by associating his own particular pain with "the Fourth of July" and "the usual debauch of patriotism" (142). He recalls how "some careless person threw a lighted cannon cracker" into the bed where he slept: "A big slice of flesh had been torn from my left shoulder; I still bear the scar." The proliferating causes for disaffection climax in a long ride in a hot packed subway train "worse than a cattle car," which immediately precedes the brief interlude of pastoral relief that the chapter title promises. In this five-page passage, the narrator's mother briefly relives her apparently idyllic childhood in rural Hungary. She walks barefoot, talks to birds, and finds appetizing brown mushrooms under trees instead of "dry, dead mushrooms in grocery stores" (152–55). Everyday constraints have been suspended for the moment: "My mother . . . looked to see if a policeman was near. There was no policeman. So she took off her shoes and stockings and walked around on the grass" (152). The mother's, and the chapter's, last words decisively deprive the narrator of such pastoral joy: " 'Ach, Got?' she said, 'I'm so happy in forest! You American children don't know what it means! I am so happy!' " Gold quickly and ironically deprived even the mother of this pastoral happiness by opening the next chapter with an image of her walking barefoot on the Chrystie Street pavement.

Like Empson, Gold understood that the pastoral treats not some remote then-and-there, but an immediate here-and-now. According to Empson, both traditional and proletarian pastoralists seek to contain or manage social and historical stresses with plain statements and clearcut images; thus the pastoral rhetorically resolves the conflicts it renders. The most influential theorist and perhaps the most successful practitioner of proletarian pastoral was the Soviet moviemaker Sergei Eisenstein, object of the most effusive tribute in Freeman's *An American Testament* (588–97). Freeman hailed Eisenstein's *The General Line* as "the first major film based on peasant material, dealing in images and in dramatic terms with problems of profound social import." Freeman praised Eisenstein for managing to make "a new social content fill an old form" and "*We* replace *I*." Freeman found in Eisenstein's films exactly those qualities that, for Empson, proletarian writing rests on. *Voices of October*, a 1930 book on early Soviet culture that Freeman cowrote, quotes Eisenstein affirming the need to reconcile "cattle and [the] tractor . . . the real hero of my new film" (240).

Gold also regarded Eisenstein as a tutelary figure. Not only did he identify Eisenstein, along with Diego Rivera, as models of proletarian realism ("Proletarian Novel"); two months later Gold told Mrs. Milton Getz, who offered to buy his typescript of *Jews Without Money*, that "there is some talk of Eisenstine [sic] doing it for a movie; if this happened, which I doubt, I would walk from here to California to swipe the manuscript back from you to hand down to my grandchildren." What Gold found most congenial in Eisenstein seems to have been his achievement in his medium of the pace and tension that Gold strove for as a prose writer, the evocation of conflict. In insisting that "proletarian realism" must involve "real conflicts" (*Anthology* 206), Gold echoed Eisenstein's dictum that "all art is conflict" (*Form* 38). "What interested Eisenstein most profoundly was the film's capacity to establish and then resolve opposites, as if it were a pictorial equivalent of Marxist historiography, as if it were emblematically synthesizing thesis and antithesis and showing the Hegelian structure underlying reality" (Shloss 152).

One measure of Gold's concern with achieving such an effect, with evoking conflict, is the extent to which "War, War" serves as a governing metaphor in *Jews Without Money* (48), as it should for proletarian art in general, according to Gold (*CW* 217). "In the summer the East Side heaven rained with potato peelings, coffee grounds, herring heads and dangerous soup bones. Bang, went a bundle, and the people in the street ducked as if a machine gun sounded" (57). Similarly, the narrator presents his mother's "German" housekeeping as "an endless frantic war with the bedbugs" (71) and identifies war with a succoring fire engine cutting through the ghetto "like a cannonball going through a regiment of soldiers" (54). Even a wind-blown snowman appears disfigured "like a war victim" (243).

The effect Gold produces in juxtaposing Fyfka the Miser and Mendel the Bum, a vividly sensory and pointedly moral clash of opposites, applies as well to scenes where no particular characters dominate (74–79). A conspicuously cinematic sequence in the chapter entitled "Summer Toadstools" includes a rapid succession of incidents. A screaming fire engine and an ambulance, the narrator and a friend debating career choices, a slow-moving scissors grinder making sparks fly all build up to the moment when "a big sightseeing bus rolled down. A gang of kids chased it, pelted rocks, garbage, dead cats and stale vegetables at the frightened sightseers. 'Liars, liars,' the kids yelled, 'go back uptown!' " (55).

After painstakingly, vividly, and (with "dead cats" sailing through the air) hyperbolically rendering this clash of opposites—uptown/downtown, frightened/bold, riders/walkers—the narrator intrudes, expressly identifying his moral and political stake in the conflict: "What right had these stuckup foreigners to come and look at us? What right had that man with the megaphone to tell them lies about us?" Gold's concern with the tour guide's megaphone is a reminder of the foremost contest in *Jews Without Money*, the one in which Gold enlisted the parrot and the goat in the opening sequence (see chapter 2)—the battle over the means of representation and cultural production.

Increasingly, the primary means of cultural production, as both Gold and Freeman knew, was the movies, the distinctly modern, mass distracting or masses mobilizing art form (Benjamin 239–40). Consequently, Gold and Freeman, both editors of the pointedly titled *New Masses* during the decades—the twenties and thirties—when the movies grew ubiquitous, sought to appropriate them. This preoccupation pervades *Never Call Retreat* where the narrator Paul Schuman recognizes "film-montage" in contrast to "a well-constructed play or an old-fashioned novel" as the only way to articulate a distinctly modern upheaval like the Nazi *Anschluss* against Austria (373). Schuman fills his prison loneliness with scenes from *It Happened One Night, Queen Christina, The Crowd,* and *The Cabinet of Dr. Caligari* (393, 511, 528). At the same time, he vacillates between honoring movies as "one of the greatest inventions of our civilization"—"the imagination on the simplest, most obvious, most universal level"—or disparaging cinema as "neurotic . . . escape" and "false refuge" (5, 528, 686, 689). This is how Schuman judges Hollywood:

I liked the films that came from Hollywood, alive with glamorous, remote figures, and those of swift meaningless deeds, which seemed to me to be the very essence of our time, until you went out of doors and found there was no thread, or only the sheerest, between the thrilling dream you just experienced with the minds of other people, filtered through the steel nerves of a machine, and the throbbing reality around you. Those films were exciting nevertheless. (356)

Then, with an evenhandedness uncharacteristic among both literary Communists and professional ex-Communists, Freeman recalled, through Schuman, the early flourishing of Soviet cinema:

so were the ones which came out of Moscow, gigantic with the luminous upsurge of other days; and the experiments with space, time, and light of the avant-garde, which had taken over several of nature's departments, not without success. Everything was there in the movie house—American romance, Russian revolution, storm over Asia, the tentative creation of new forms; worlds of fantasy wherein you could lose yourself for hours and live through imagined victories of love and beauty and justice, swiftly, intensely, and always vicariously.

While working on *Never Call Retreat*, Freeman published an essay entitled "Biographical Films" on the spate of biographies Hollywood produced in the thirties: *Northwest Passage, Zola, Juarez, Sergeant York, Abe Lincoln in Illinois, Young Tom Edison, Mayerling*, and finally, *Citizen Kane*. Each "centered men's thoughts on the historic process and the historic hero" and "the problem of power" (902, 906). In these movies "the conflicts of private life are replaced in part by those of the body politic" (900). In *Never Call Retreat*, Freeman seems to have emulated this Hollywood model. Like his alter ego Paul Schuman, Freeman credited this "product of the turbulent Thirties" with having "alter[ed] attitudes toward history . . . revolution and counter-revolution, invasion and civil war, the collapse of an economic system and the dissolution of an entire culture" (902).

Gold was also preoccupied with Hollywood; for example, he once savaged Shirley Temple as "a movie monkey" in a "humid hothouse" (*CW* 169–72). This preoccupation had been a staple of American Communist Kulturkampf as early as the 1920s. Freeman remembers cartoonist Robert Minor proposing a "story on POISON IN THE MOVIES or THE MOVIE MAGNATES' STRANGLE-HOLD, or something like that—description of the filth factories in Hollywood which have killed off every spark of life in the popular theaters of America—which have shut off the development of a great art—potentially; which have destroyed all the individuality in production as well as all public freedom of choice" (*AT* 319). Published in 1926, one of Gold's earliest *New Masses* pieces, "Faster, America, Faster!" was subtitled "a movie in ten reels" and shaped like a silent movie screenplay (*Anthology* 140–47). This apocalyptic satire shows, in montagelike cross section, a private train belonging to Schmidt, a Hollywood mogul. Gold's script keeps cutting from the "Hollywood-ing" of the passengers—their conspicuous consumption and hysterical hedonism—and the frantic efforts of the locomotive crew to keep the train accelerating (as the revelers command) to the "Negroes in the pantry" who hope that "the old ofay busts a blood vessel." In structuring this attack on Hollywood according to Hollywood convention, Gold was striving transparently to use the means of cultural production in order to seize them. Hence Gold's only other book-length composition, besides *Jews Without Money, Charlie Chaplin's Parade*, a children's book published in 1930, also drew on Hollywood.

In view of such attempts to take his Kulturkampf to the movies and in view of Gold's insistence that proletarian realism had to be "cinema in words," Leslie Fiedler's intended insult, his comparison labeling Gold "the Al Jolson of the Communist movement," may justly evoke the crudity and vulgarity for which Gold has been so loudly condemned (Gold, *Anthology* 207; Fiedler, *Jewish* 31). But, as much as he ridiculed their failings, Fiedler may also have unwittingly described Gold's and his movement's goal. Murray Kempton conceded the realization of this goal, by retrospectively and snobbishly disparaging the migration "into radio or Hollywood" of the "social muse" that Gold's and Freeman's Kulturkampf promoted (139). In a 1937 col-

umn, entitled "Notes on the Cultural Front," Gold wel-
comed this Kulturkampf migration and honored the success "of proletarian pioneers" in altering the mass media:
"When Hollywood present[ed] plays like *Dead End*," it was
"unconsciously acknowledging the national victory of literary ideas whose champions ten years ago could only be
found in the pages of the *Masses*" (4).

For the literary left, the city, along with the commerce
and industry that it fostered and depended on, posed the
problem of modernity at least as much as the movies did.
"Next to that of the motion pictures," according to Gold,
stood architecture as the art "that reaches the greatest
masses of people" (*CW* 151). In a 1926 art show review for
the *Daily Worker*, Freeman announced that "the prophetic
eyes of Marx foresaw that art could not long escape the
effects of machinery and the factory system" ("Revolutionary"). Gold's recurrent and troubled attention to the urban
skyline and his antagonism to the industrial development
known derogatorily as Fordism reveal how much cities
and factories vexed the literary left. Not only did the
growth of cities lie at center of the rapid modernizing that
took place over the past two centuries but "the look of the
city" contributed consequentially to the development of
modernism in literature and the visual arts (Roeder 63).
The look of the city preoccupied Gold as a typically divided modernist and also as a partisan ideologue, an aesthete and a moralist, persistent in showing how "people
are bigger than skyscrapers" (qtd. in Shields 50): "We may
use skyscrapers under Communism, but they will be built
to answer the people's needs. Under capitalism they are
only weapons of exploitation and the vulgarization of life"
(*CW* 153). Serving as "the abstract, universal sign of capitalism" and "as the utopian form to end all others," skyscrapers stood for industrialism by honoring "the image of
the machine" (Hughes 198).

Gold's 1927 play, *Hoboken Blues*, which tells the story of
an unsuccessful Harlem job seeker, pointedly evokes the
look of the city, the troubling meanings of the skyline and
its underlying industrialism (603–5). Gold's plotting in the

play contrasts the contemporary cityscape to that of the turn of the century—when *Jews Without Money* is set—with a mixture of horror and fascination. Stage directions call for "the same cross-section of tenement as in the first act, but vastly angular, confusing, colorful, and jazzy; a composition of sharp, outrageous lines, an ensemble of militant statements by a drunken geometrician. . . . Industrialism rampant. . . . Advertising signs are scattered over the buildings and swung from the sky." The action of this scene begins when a "funny little Ford car rolls in," driven by character Gold named the "Fordist," whom the cop on the beat dismisses with "run along now, Henry Ford."

Gold's brand-name specificity anticipates a 1934 column entitled "Henry Ford's Inferno." Here Gold set out to unmask "the myth of Fordism . . . as an answer to Communism" (*CW* 195). Fordism, according to Gold, governed cultural production as well as heavy industry, as Gold's Chaplinesque vision of the Hollywood assembly line illustrates:

It's a dream world, where everything comes out all right in the end. It's a world that makes myths, that creates heroes . . . a huge factory where the human emotions are manufactured. Tears, sighs, longings, desires, successes, are turned out as you assemble a Ford in the Detroit plants. Like a huge belt, Hollywood has divided its workers like the workers on a conveyor. (*CW* 140)

Ford himself Gold cast as "a moody despot with a mind more provincial than that of the most barbarous village bigot" (*CW* 17; *Reader* 92).* Though it echoes the disparagement of *dem Idiotismus des Landlebens*—the seclusion, ignorance, and barbarism of rural life—in *The Communist Manifesto*, Gold's snobbery toward the "village" and the provinces is puzzling in view of his ongoing pastoral critique of modernity. This critique focused synecdochically on the skyscraper as an emblem of the misrepresented and

---

* Revised in the fifties for *The Mike Gold Reader*, bigot replaced "Baptist" (cf. Freeman, *AT* 17, 161).

destructive "progress" that the modern city produces. As early as 1921, reporting elegiacally on anarchist "colonists" in rural New Jersey, Gold pronounced pastorally that "the cities hold them down" however much they try "to live the good life" (*Anthology* 73). Thus the cop in *Hoboken Blues* goes on from his dismissal of the Fordist to deprecate a "hoss-cah philosopher" who also witnessed the Fordist's advent by describing the fate of the horse car: "It wuz pushed from the sixtieth floor of a skyscraper. . . . An aeroplane bombed it to pieces." The moral meaning of skyscrapers in Gold's demonology seems evident in "Down with Skyscrapers," one of Gold's *Daily Worker* columns, which denounced the "damned monstrous skyscrapers . . . rigged up hastily by greedy land speculators" instead of by and for the people (*CW* 153).

Here Gold mines a vein opened by the most remembered American foreseer of his era, Lincoln Steffens, who "saw the future" in the Soviet Union in the 1920s and memorably pronounced that "it works." Some twenty years earlier, when Gold was still a boy, Steffens questioned

climbing skylines writing with reckless realism across the heavens the same great story of material progress. It is time to read the writing on the walls. It may mean more than the increase of wealth, the growing power of capital, the might of skilled and disciplined labor. These have their own value, and have been the cause of national pride, but now they are the scapegoats of reactionary discontent. (37)

This view of antipathy to skyscrapers as "reactionary discontent" calls into question the ideological consistency, the partisan purity, of Gold's own denunciations, unless we read them more as a typically modernist aversion toward modernity than as a Marxist embrace of industrialization and urbanization. In Gold's denunciation of modernity, the rhetoric of pastoral lament prevails: "I would wager that two-thirds of the New York workers would give all the skyscrapers in the world for a little shack in the country, and a chance for their babies to breathe pure, clean air" (*CW* 154). Attacks on skyscrapers and Fordism pervade Gold's writing. Thus "Henry Ford's Inferno" compares Ford himself to Caligula and Fordism to Nazism (*CW* 197). In 1940, Gold described the twenties as "the boom period, when the hero of liberal intellectuals was Henry Ford; when poets and artists became mystical about skyscrapers, bridges, and the mere noise, smoke and dirt of factory towns" (*Anthology* 273).

Just before publishing *Hoboken Blues*, in 1927, Gold published a manifesto in the *New Masses*, reminiscent of Shelley's "Defense of Poetry" or Emerson's "The Poet," entitled "America Needs a Critic." Its anaphoric conclusion implored "Life" to "send America a great literary critic":

Send a strong poet who loves the masses, and their future. Send someone who doesn't give a damn about money. Send one who is not a pompous liberal, but a man of the street. Send no mystics—they give Americans the willies. Send no coward. Send no pedant. Send us a man to stand up to *skyscrapers*. A man of art who can match the purposeful deeds of *Henry Ford*. Send us a joker in overalls. Send no saint. Send an artist. Send a scientist. Send a Bolshevik. Send a man. (*Anthology* 138–39; emphases added).

Striking in this passage is the opposition between the "future," identified with the masses, and the past, implicitly identified with Fordism and skyscrapers. This opposition contrasts markedly with the prevailing progressive view of "factories and skyscrapers" as "the emblematic symbols of the new culture" (Bell 125). In a late autobiographical sketch entitled "The Writer in America" Gold maintained this critique-by-synecdoche by associating skyscrapers with the 1914 "unemployment crisis in which I was a victim" for whom the loss "of a job was a tragedy that loomed bigger than all the proud skyscrapers" (*Reader* 181). Yet in most of Gold's autobiographical narratives, in contrast to his more overtly critical work, skyscrapers either take on a sentimental cast or show Gold torn between a favorable, conventionally capitalist image of the modern skyline and his polemic, as a moralist, against it.

In "A Jewish Childhood," Gold recalled that to come out onto the roof "was always glorious" with "the sun setting in red and gold on the Jersey shore! The skyscrapers flaming in the sunset!" (303). As much a Romantic moralist as a Marxist, Gold voiced here the paradoxically modernist-antimodern stance that Alan Trachtenberg traces back to Adams's *Education* and to "City of Ambition" by Alfred Stieglitz, "whose civic-minded outcry for control" joined in this photograph with "Stieglitz's self-declared alienation from commercial forces thrusting the city higher and higher, reshaping the city according to the forces of the marketplace" (216–17). Perhaps the most famous romantic-moralistic skyline image in American writing comes in chapter 4 of *The Great Gatsby*, where Fitzgerald balances an iconographic skyline view of "the city seen for the first time" with sarcastic iconoclasm, "the city rising up across the river in white heaps and sugar lumps all built with a wish out of nonolfactory money."

Gold's densest skyline images, which appear in *Jews Without Money*, similarly blend nostalgic moralistic censure with hopeful, complicit fascination. Such images figure with particular resonance in the narrator's recollections of his father—a wannabe millionaire and defeated pursuer of the conventionally capitalist American dream (215, 301–2). Thus the father tells his son, the narrator, how as a boy in Romania his first vicarious view of America, the picture that began to draw him there, showed America as the land of mass-produced machinery and vertical cityscapes: "I had seen two pictures of America. They were shown in the window of a store that sold Singer sewing machines in our village. One picture had in it the tallest building I had ever seen. It was called a skyscraper. At the bottom of it walked the proud Americans. The men wore derby hats and had fine mustaches and gold watch chains. The women wore silks and satins, and had proud faces like queens. . . . Everyone was rich" (102). Once in America, these skyscrapers stand at an immutable remove from the father's own opportunities, a backdrop to and a humiliating reminder of his own grandiose delusions and recurring setbacks. Thus the narrator describes his father staging his storytelling sessions on the roof of their tenement: "He smoked a cigar. Behind him stood a cardboard jumble of tenement chimneys and skyscrapers," which "hung like tall ships with red and white lamps . . . up against the moon" (84, 87).

Later on, the narrator befriends a funeral wagon driver. Transporting corpses to Brooklyn, they "ride across the Brooklyn Bridge, with the incredible sweep of New York below us" (271). Awed by the vista, the narrator misses the chastening, sobering point of the trip: "The river was packed tight, a street with tugboat traffic . . . mammoth skyscrapers cut the sky like a saw. The smoke of factories smeared the bright blue air. Horns boomed and wailed; Brooklyn lay low and passive in the horizon." This vibrant panorama and the narrator's enthusiasm, however, follow and precede scenes of actual grieving for the deceased in the wagon, at home in Manhattan and at the graveyard in Brooklyn. The narrator apparently allows himself to forget for a moment the gravity of the circumstances while Gold's framing of this scene keeps this grimmer information before the reader.

The precariousness of the resulting Whitmanesque Brooklyn crossing idyll, a simultaneously elegiac and rhapsodic tour de force, quickly becomes evident. This chapter, entitled "Blood Money," builds carefully to the melodramatic climax of the novel, the killing of the narrator's sister Esther under the wheels of a freight wagon. The accident takes place on a winter day when "the world was dark" with only "stores and skyscrapers . . . illuminated. . . . The saloons blazing with gas and electricity" (277). Commerce and industry tempt and deceive, casting the tenement into darkness by exercising a monopoly on light and on the heat that Esther was looking for on her last errand, "to gather wood for the stove" (278).

As in *The Great Gatsby,* such recurring skyscraper images appear at a distance. Through this distance, the viewer-narrator domesticates his fascination with and disapproval of the snares of commerce and industry; rhapsody and censure reciprocally contain each other. Gold's narrator literally distances himself from the falsely glamorous promise of self-enrichment and self-advancement that the Manhattan skyline conventionally makes.

All this iconoclasm and suspicion toward the skyline and toward industrialism run counter to the emulatory appropriation of American industrialism, especially Fordism, by early Soviet leaders. According to Warren Sussman, Fordism "was hailed in the 1920s as a major contribution to twentieth-century revolution by Marxists as imposing as Vladimir Lenin," so that "it was not at all unusual to find Ford's portrait hanging alongside that of Lenin in Soviet factories" (132). Such sentiments also run counter to the faith in engineering for all life, its "intangible" as well its material "base," that Soviet-sponsored Communism held to under Stalin, whose view of "writers as engineers of the human soul" Gold honored (*CW* 154). Edmund Wilson examined this principle in describing "the Marxist vision of Lenin" as "a creation, not of literary art, but of actual social engineering" whereby "society itself . . . becomes the work of art" (*Triple* 288–89). Gold's and Wilson's invocation of the engineer points metonymically to distinctly modern claims that we can exercise technological control over formerly mysterious forces of nature and, according to Marxists, over the oppressing classes' mystified and mystifying instruments of pseudonature. At the same time, such engineering displaces, moots, the visionary authority and the cultural privilege of the literati, which rests paradoxically on the romantic "individualism that underlies Marx's communism" (M. Berman 127–28).

Both Gold and Freeman tried to talk themselves and their readers out of the romantic opposition between technology—engineering and machinery—and individual expression, the cultural freedom that romanticisms affirm. Freeman began *An American Testament* by describing himself as having come "at seven from a little Ukrainian village to the metropolis of America and [having] shuddered at the stone monsters stretching to the sky" (16). He later learned that his stress was "a common experience . . .

more or less universal." After visiting the same anarchist commune in New Jersey, in 1921, that Gold reported on in "A Little Bit of Millenium" (*Anthology* 71–79), Freeman belittled their anti-industrial principles as merely "aesthetic" (*AT* 288):

They damned the machine age, although this damnation was compensatory, since many of them worked at machines in the clothing factories of New York. Surrounded by the most mechanized and industrialized country in the world . . . they were, spiritually at least, machine-wreckers. . . . Art was not an attempt to express contemporary civilization, but to escape from it into dreams of a nonindustrial world assumed to be full of peace, beauty and love. . . . They sought a Europe of the past . . . not . . . the Ruhr or Manchester . . . or an Orient which never existed . . . in Mexico a past which the agrarian revolution and American imperialism were rapidly wiping out. The intellectual suffered from a nostalgia . . . for the golden pastoral age. (289)

Freeman argued that his own background as an immigrant freed him from such nostalgia. Examining Freeman's milieu, Hutchins Hapgood sorted out three conflicting strands of influence in this background: Jewish, American, Socialist (18).

The little Jewish boy finds himself in contact with a new world which stands in violent contrast with the orthodox environment of his first few years. . . . He achieves a growing comprehension and sympathy with the independent, free, rather skeptical spirit of the American boy . . . ideas about social equality and contempt for authority. . . . Socialism as it is agitated in the Jewish quarter consists in a wholesale rejection, founded on a misunderstanding, of both American and Hebraic ideals . . . that the old religion is rubbish and that American institutions were invented to exploit the workingman. The natural effects . . . are . . . a tendency to look with distrust at the genuinely American life . . . and to reject the old implicit piety. (23, 24, 34)

Freeman described the consequences of such an upbringing as "living too many lives" and called upon himself "to live in the twentieth century, to erase all traces of the vanished village, the Middle Ages, the church bells

. . . the shadows of the pogrom . . . the isolation of an immigrant boy" (*AT* 655). The conflict between these strains, Freeman insisted, was especially enabling: "From the medieval village I brought a fresh viewpoint. . . . In this hostile, weird world, I had to change my whole life . . . to examine, experiment with, accept or reject" (15). As a result of "the warring cultures which struggled within me for dominance," Freeman believed that he could share critically in the modernist censure of modernity, immune from the reactionary modernists' susceptibility to nostalgia. Freeman's distinction, he claimed, lay in the movement he experienced over the course of his life, "from candle to kerosene to gaslight to electricity . . . stinking ditches and wooden sidewalks" in the Ukraine "to the modern sewage and asphalt of New York" (289), from a "medieval" culture (289, 15, vii), the persistence of which the New York-born Gold also encountered as a boy on the Lower East Side (*Jews Without Money* 143). From Freeman's perspective, such changes "looked like progress" and made him admittedly " 'bourgeois' " inasmuch as he "preferred shoes to sandals" (*AT* 289):

I remembered the vanished village of my childhood and with it the defects of preindustrial life. There was peace in the fields, there was also poverty, ignorance, pogroms . . . I could not romanticize the impoverished, drab life of the preindustrial world which I knew; instead, I romanticized the machine, which was for me as much an abstraction as the European or Mexican village was for the tourists. . . . This abstraction . . . had its value; it rendered me susceptible to the Marxist explanation of the machine." (289)

As Freeman goes on to explain, the Marxist Kulturkampf requires an appropriation of the machine, a redefinition and revaluation of its meaning whereby the "the capitalist use" of machines and its cruel "results" differ from the socialist use of technology and its results: "a higher standard of living . . . universal leisure . . . the development and spread of art . . . the free development of the individual"

Like Woody Guthrie, who declared his acoustic guitar a fascist-killing "machine," Gold simply decreed the triumph of this transvaluation: "The machine! The machine! Surely every thoughtful high-school student knows by now that the machine is a monster only under individual exploitation, but is destined to become the mother of a great democratic culture, with peace and plenty for all, when it has become collectivized" ("Mabel" 12).

In this deferment of modernity into an indefinite but inevitably democratic future lies Gold's and Freeman's romantic and Marxist strategy of containment. Similarly, the transformation of the machine from monster to mother dissolves the conventional distinction between (mother) nature and human-made culture. Such strategies obscured the impasse to which their Marxist modernism brought them.

The impossibility of at once rendering and managing change kept Freeman and Gold, like the canonic modernists they challenged and emulated, from dissolving the opacity of history and from transcending the given, even rhetorically. Freeman's and Gold's tenacious and contradictory engagements with modernity result in the same sort of repression of history that Fredric Jameson ascribes to "the poetic apparatus of high modernism" (*Political* 280). Hence even Gold's most iconoclastic invocations of iconic skyscrapers reinforces their iconic status. Likewise, even Freeman's subversive adaptation of the conversion narrative legacy derived from Adams and Augustine upholds the form and blunts Freeman's subversive motive, whatever radical consequence he may have intended. Furthermore, the repercussions that *An American Testament* provoked entirely effaced revealing questions of form and rhetoric, displacing them with more narrowly topical and partisan concerns. Consequently, the processes of cultural production that Gold and Freeman set out to illuminate and so master remain opaque throughout their writing.

Each effort to render politics, the historical conditions and economic events that produce history, makes the politics treated seem, in retrospect, more aesthetic and more mystified rather than less. As Walter Benjamin observed, war—apparently including culture war—necessitates turning politics aesthetic (241). This inevitability helps account for the mystifying, idealizing, and aestheticizing that Gold's and Freeman's literary Marxism—contrary to their agenda—entailed.

Consequently a recoil into idealism and not some conceptually and formally new way of embracing materialism ends each writer's most significant book. Even though he enclosed "ideal" and "ideals" in quotation marks, Freeman's repetition of the word four times in as many sentences imposes on his reader a dichotomous choice between the "two colossal social 'ideals'" of "our age": "Fascism . . . and socialism, or the utmost imaginable freedom for the mass of humanity" (*AT* 668). Freeman's extravagance here (in his adjectives "colossal" and "utmost") evaporates the skepticism that his quotation marks around "ideal" signal.

Likewise, in *Jews Without Money*, the narrator ends his story by simultaneously opening and closing his mind. First he identifies the ideal of a "worker's revolution" as "the true messiah" and a sentence later he insists that this coercive messianism, a mythic solution rather than a skeptical revision, "forced me to think" (309). The contradiction—between "force" and "thought"—belongs to the effort to solicit intellectually, as Gold and Freeman did, the "messianic cessation" that Walter Benjamin envisioned:

Thinking involves not only the flow of thoughts, but their arrest as well. Where thinking suddenly stops in a configuration pregnant with tensions, it gives the configuration a shock, by which it crystallizes into a monad. A historical materialist approaches a historical subject only where he encounters it as a monad. In this structure, he recognizes the sign of a Messianic cessation of happening, a revolutionary chance in the fight for an oppressed past. (263)

This "fight," the Kulturkampf that Freeman and Gold waged, continues. If we can't recognize our culture wars in Gold's and Freeman's, then our current struggles will soon seem just as opaque or irrelevant as theirs have—wrongly—seemed to many readers. Recognizing our links with Gold and Freeman, however, will enable us to claim and use their legacy, instead of dismissing or deforming it out of the fear and condescension that has colored many past readings of their work. These efforts will involve settling the sort of historical claims that Benjamin described: "There is a secret agreement between past generations and the present one. Our coming was expected on earth. Like every generation that preceded us, we have been endowed with a *weak* Messianic power, a power to which the past has a claim. That claim cannot be settled cheaply. Historical materialists are aware of that" (Benjamin 254).

This study of Gold and Freeman has tried to maintain this historical materialist awareness by articulating the claims that Benjamin described and that Gold and Freeman helped to construct and may, if my readings persuade, become increasingly identified with.

I hope that I have made the implications of these claims for the study and the production of literature apparent and that I have enabled readers to read Gold's and Freeman's work and appreciate their careers more justly. My intent has been to examine, as a participant in the culture wars we can't avoid, the resources at our disposal and to learn from Freeman's and Gold's achievements and failures how to struggle more wisely and more charitably. Finally, the most important part of this project for me has been the opportunity to reconstruct and inhabit Gold's and Freeman's efforts to make fiction and poetry and criticism out of their shared passion for justice. Underlying this book is the assumption that we belittle such efforts—however crude, however "vulgar"—only at our greatest peril.

George Steiner, surprisingly, honored Bertolt Brecht, perhaps the most influential Communist writer contemporary with Freeman and Gold, by praising such generously mistaken writers as Freeman, Gold, and Brecht:

Those who were wrong, hideously wrong, like the Bolsheviks, the Communards in France in 1871, the International Brigades in the Spanish Civil War, the millions who died proclaiming their fidelity to Stalin were, in a paradoxical, profoundly tragic way, less wrong than the clairvoyant, than the ironists and yuppies, than the Madison Avenue hype peddlers and jobbers. . . . It is better to have to have been hallucinated by justice than to have been awakened to junk food. (114)

At a time when so much of our politics, left and right, has become a medium of self-congratulation and so much of our criticism capitalizes on exploiting difference, Freeman's and Gold's "hallucinations," contradictions, and intellectual impasses may prove especially instructive.

# Works Cited

## Abbreviations

FREEMAN: *AT = An American Testament.*
*LP = The Long Pursuit. NCR = Never Call Retreat.*
GOLD: *CW = Change the World. HM = The Hollow Men. J = Jews Without Money.*
OTHER: *BRD = Book Review Digest.*

## Collections

Joseph Freeman Papers, Hoover Institution for War, Revolution, and Peace, Stanford University.

Michael Gold Papers, Fales Collection, Bobst Library, New York University.

Charmion Von Wiegand Papers, Archives of American Art, Smithsonian Institute.

Paper of Theodore Dreiser, Horace Liveright, and Lewis Mumford, Van Pelt Library, University of Pennsylvania.

Aaron, Daniel. *Writers on the Left.* 1951. New York: Avon, 1969.

Aaron Daniel et al. "Symposium: Thirty Years Later—Memories of the First American Writers' Congress." *American Scholar* (1966), 35(3): 495–509.

Abrams, M. H. *Natural Supernaturalism: Tradition and Revolution in Romantic Literature.* 1971. New York: Norton, 1973.

Adams, Henry. *The Education of Henry Adams*. 1918. New York, Modern Library, 1931.

Arac, Jonathan. *Critical Genealogies: Historical Situations for Postmodern Literary Study*. New York: Columbia University Press, 1989.

Arnowitz, Stanley. *The Crisis in Historical Materialism: Class, Politics, and Culture in Marxist Theory*. New York: Praeger, 1981.

Baker, Houston. "Caliban's Triple Play." In H. L. Gates, ed., *"Race," Writing, and Difference*, pp. 381–95. Chicago: University of Chicago Press, 1986.

Bakhtin, Mikhail. *The Dialogic Imagination*. Trs. Michael Holquist and Caryl Emerson. Austin: University of Texas Press, 1981.

Beck, Kent. "The Odyssey of Joseph Freeman." *The Historian* (November 1974), 37(1): 101–120.

Bell, Daniel. "Modernism Mummified." *American Quarterly* (1987), 39(1): 122–132.

Bender, Thomas. *New York Intellect*. New York: Knopf, 1987.

Benjamin, Walter. *Illuminations: Essays and Reflections*. Tr. Harry Zohn. New York: Schocken, 1985.

Bercovitch, Sacvan. *The American Jeremiad*. Madison: University of Wisconsin Press, 1982.

Berger, John. *The Success and Failure of Picasso*. 1965. New York: Penguin, 1966.

Berkhofer, Robert. "A New Context for Am Studies" *American Quarterly* (December 1989), 41(4):588–613

Berman, Marshall. *All That Is Solid Melts into Air: The Experience of Modernity*. New York: Simon and Schuster, 1982.

Berman, Paul. "East Side Story: Mike Gold, the Communists and the Jews." *Voice Literary Supplement* (March 1983), pp. 9–13.

Bogardus, Ralph and Fred Hobson. Introduction to *Literature at the Barricades: The American Writer in the 1930s*, pp. 1–12. Montgomery: University of Alabama Press, 1982.

*Book Review Digest: 1930*. Ed. Marion Knight et al. New York: H. W. Wilson, 1931.

*Book Review Digest: 1936*. Eds. Mertice James, Dorothy Brown. New York: H. W. Wilson, 1936.

*Book Review Digest: 1943*. Eds. Mertice James, Dorothy Brown. New York: H. W. Wilson, 1943.

*Book Review Digest: 1947*. Eds. Mertice James, Dorothy Brown. New York: H. W. Wilson, 1947.

Bromwich, David. *A Choice of Inheritance: Self and Community from*

*Edmund Burke to Robert Frost*. Cambridge: Harvard University Press, 1988.

Burke, Kenneth. *Attitudes Toward History*. 1937. Boston: Beacon, 1961.

—— *A Grammar of Motives*. 1945. Berkeley: University of California Press, 1969

—— "The Writers Congress." *The Nation* (May 15, 1935), p. 573.

Cahan, Abraham. *The Rise of David Levinsky*. 1917. New York: Harper Colophon, 1966.

Callahan, John F. "Becoming a Citizen in the 'Country of Language': Storytelling and the Scholarly Voice in *The Book of Daniel*." In *The Green American Tradition: Essays and Poems for Sherman Paul*, pp. 245–256. Baton Rouge: Louisiana State University Press, 1989.

Calverton, V. F. *The Liberation of American Literature*. 1932. New York: Farrar Straus, 1973.

Casciato, Arthur. "Citizen Writers: A History of the League of American Writers, 1935–42." Ph.D. diss. University of Virginia, 1986.

Castonovo, David. *Thornton Wilder*. New York: Ungar, 1986.

Concha, Jaime. Preface. In Neil Larsen, *Modernism and Hegemony: A Materialist Critique of Agency*, pp. ix–xxi. Minneapolis: University of Minnesota Press, 1990.

Conroy, Frank. *The Disinherited*. 1933. New York: Farrar Straus/ Hill & Wang, 1963.

Cooper, Wayne. *Claude McKay: Rebel Sojourner in the Harlem Renaissance*. Baton Rouge: Louisiana State University Press, 1987.

Cowley, Malcolm. *—And I Worked at the Writer's Trade: Chapters of Literary History: 1918–1978*. New York: Viking, 1978.

—— *The Dream of the Golden Mountains: Remembering the 1930s*. Viking, 1980.

—— *Think Back On Us: A Contemporary Chronicle of the 1930s*. Ed. Henry Dan Piper. Carbondale: Southern Illinois University Press, 1967.

Craig, Gordon. *Germany 1866–1945*. New York: Oxford, 1978.

Dawidowicz, Lucy. *From That Place and Time: Memoirs, 1938–47*. New York: Norton, 1989.

Dickstein, Morris. "Hallucinating the Past: *Jews Without Money* Revisited." *Grand Street* (Winter 1989) 9(2): 155–168.

—— "The Tenement and the World: Visions of Immigrant Life." In William Boelhower, ed., *The Future of American Modernism*, pp. 62–92. Amsterdam: VU University Press, 1990.

Doctorow, E. L. *The Book of Daniel*. 1971. New York: Fawcett, 1987.

Doherty, Thomas. "American Autobiography and Ideology." In Albert Stone, *The American Autobiography: A Collection of Essays*, pp. 95–108. Englewood Cliffs, N.J.: Prentice Hall, 1981.

Donald, David H. *Look Homeward: A Life of Thomas Wolfe*. Boston: Little, Brown, 1987.

Dowling, William. *Jameson, Althusser, and Marx: An Introduction to The Political Unconscious*. Ithaca: Cornell University Press, 1984.

Draper, Theodore. *The Roots of American Communism*. New York: Viking, 1957.

Duberman, Martin. *Paul Robeson*. New York: Knopf, 1989.

Eastman, Max. *Artists in Uniform*. New York: Knopf, 1934.

—— *Love and Revolution*. New York: Random House, 1964.

Eistenstein, Sergei. *Film Form: Essays in Film Theory*. Tr. Jay Leyda. Harcourt, 1949.

Eliot, George. *Felix Holt, Radical*. 1866. London: Penguin, 1972.

Eliot, T. S. *The Use of Poetry and the Use of Criticism*. 1933. London: Faber, 1968.

Empson, William. *Some Versions of Pastoral*. 1935: London: Chatto & Windus, 1950.

Farrell, James. *A Note on Literary Criticism*. New York: Vanguard, 1936.

Fiedler, Leslie. *The Jew in the American Novel*. New York: Herzl Institute, 1959.

—— *The Stranger in Shakespeare*. New York: Stein & Day 1972.

Folsom, Michael. "The Book of Poverty" *The Nation* (February 28), pp. 242–45.

—— "The Education of Mike Gold." In David Madden, ed., *Proletarian Writers in the Thirties*, pp. 222–251. Carbondale, Southern Illinois University Press, 1968.

Foucault, Michel. *Language, Counter-Memory, Practice: Selected Essays and Interviews*. Tr. Donald Bouchard. Ithaca: Cornell University Press, 1977.

Franklin, H. Bruce. "Teaching Literature in the Higher Academies of the Empire." In Louis Kampf and Paul Lauter, eds., *The Politics of Literature: Dissenting Essays in the Teaching of English*, New York: Pantheon, 1972.

Freeman, Joseph. *An American Testament*. New York: Farrar Rinehart, 1936.

—— "Biographical Films" *Theater Arts Monthly* (December 1941), pp. 900–906.

—— "Critics in Mufti." *New Masses* (May 5, 1929).

—— "The Forbidden Tree." Ms. 1954. Hoover, box 172.

—— "From the Finland Station." Ms. n.d. Hoover, box 122.

—— "God Sees the Truth." *Harper's* (April 1941), pp. 542–548.

—— Introduction. In Granville Hicks et al., eds., *Proletarian Literature in the United States*, pp. 9–28. New York: International, 1935.

—— "Ivory Towers—Red and White." *New Masses* (September 1934), pp. 20–24.

—— "Literary Theories." *New Masses* (May 1929): pp. 12–13.

—— *The Long Pursuit*. New York: Rinehart, 1947.

—— "Mask Image Truth." *Partisan Review* (1938), nos. 7 and 8, pp. 3–17.

—— *Never Call Retreat*. New York: Farrar Rinehart, 1943.

—— "A Note on Henry Adams." Ms. 1923–24. Hoover, box 89.

—— "Realism and American Fiction." Ms. 1926. Hoover, box. 89.

—— "Revolutionary Artist." *Daily Worker* (March 21), 1926. Ms. Hoover, box 29.

—— "Russia and the U.S." *Life* (August 27, 1945).

—— "Social Trends in American Literature." *The Communist* (July 1930). Ms. Hoover, box 89.

—— "Toward the Forties," In Henry Hart, ed., *The Writer in a Changing World*, pp. 9–33. New York, Equinox Cooperative, 1937.

—— "The Vision of the Thirties." Lecture at Smith College, May 7, 1958. Reprint "From *The Grecourt Review*" n.d., n.p.

—— "The Wilsonian Era in American Literature." *Modern Quarterly* (June-Sept 1927), pp. 130–136.

Freeman, Joseph, Joshua Kunitz, and Louis Lozowick. *Voices of October: Art and Literature in Soviet Russia*. New York: Vanguard, 1930.

Fussell, Paul. *Abroad: Literary Travel Between the Wars*. New York: Oxford University Press, 1980.

—— *The Great War and Modern Memory*. New York: Oxford University Press, 1975.

Gilbert, James. "Literature and Revolution in the United States" *Journal of Contemporary History* (1967), 2(2): 161–76.

—— *Writers and Partisans: A History of Literary Radicalism in America: 1900–50*. New York: Wiley, 1968.

Gitlin, Todd. Hip-Deep in Postmodernism. *New York Times Book Review* Nov. 6, 1988.

—— *The Sixties: Years of Hope, Days of Rage.* New York: Bantam, 1987.

Godine, Amy. "Notes Toward a Reappraisal of Depression Literature," *Prospects* (1980), vol. 5.

Gold, Michael. *Change the World.* New York: International, 1936.

—— *Charlie Chaplin's Parade.* New York: Harcourt, 1930.

—— "Hoboken Blues." In Lewis Mumford, ed., *The American Caravan.* New York: Macauley, 1927.

—— *The Hollow Men.* New York: International, 1941.

—— "Let It Be Really New." *New Masses* (June 1926), pp. 20–26.

—— *Jews Without Money.* 1930. New York: Carroll & Graf, 1984.

—— *Life of John Brown.* 1923. New York: Roving Eye, 1960.

*Mike Gold: A Literary Anthology.* Ed. Michael Folsom. New York: International, 1972.

*The Mike Gold Reader.* Ed. Samuel Sillen. New York: International, 1954.

—— "Mabel Luhan's Slums." *New Masses* (Sept. 1, 1936) pp. 11–14.

—— "Notes on the Cultural Front." *New Masses* (December 7, 1937), pp. 1–5.

—— "A Proletarian Novel?" Letter to *New Republic* (June 4, 1930), p. 74.

—— "What a World: William Carlos Williams." *Daily Worker* (October 12, 1933).

Gornick, Vivian. *The Romance of American Communism.* New York: Basic, 1977.

Gramsci, Antonio. "Marxism and Modern Culture." In *The Modern Prince and Other Essays,* pp. 82–89. Tr. Louis Marx. New York: International, 1957.

Greenblatt, Stephen. "Learning to Curse: Aspects of Linguistic Colonialism in the Sixteenth Century." In Fredi Chiapelli, ed., *First Images of America: The Impact of the New World on the Old,* 2:561–580. 2 vols. Berkeley: University of California Press, 1976.

—— *Shakespearian Negotiations: The Circulation of Social Energy in Renaissance England.* Berkeley: University of California Press, 1986.

Grossberger, Lewis. "The Rush Hours." *New York Times Magazine* (December 16, 1990), pp. 58, 92–96.

Guttmann, Allen. *The Jewish Writer in America: Assimilation and the Crisis of Identity.* New York: Oxford University Press, 1971.

Hapgood, Hutchins. *The Spirit of the Ghetto.* 1902. Ed. Moses Rischin. Cambridge: Harvard University Press, 1967.

Hart, Henry, ed. *The American Writers Congress*. New York: International, 1935.

—— *The Writer in a Changing World*. New York: Equinox Cooperative, 1937.

Hartman, Geoffrey. *Saving the Text: Literature/Derrida/Philosophy*. Baltimore: John Hopkins University Press, 1981.

Hassan, Ihab. "Fictions of Power: A Note on Ideological Discourse in the Humanities." *American Literary History* (Spring 1989), 1:131–142.

Hatlen, Burton. "Why Is *The Education of Henry Adams* 'Literature' While *The Theory of the Leisure Class* Is Not?" *College English* (February 1979), 40(6): 665–676.

Herbst, Josephine. "Yesterday's Road." In Ralph Bogardus and Fred Hobson, eds., *Literature at the Barricades*, pp. 29–45. Montgomery: University of Alabama Press, 1982.

Hicks, Granville. *The Great Tradition: An Interpretation of American Literature Since the Civil War*. New York: Macmillan, 1983.

Hicks, Granville et al., eds. *Proletarian Literature in the United States*. New York: International, 1935.

Hofstadter, Richard. *Anti-Intellectualism in American Life*. 1962. New York: Vintage, 1963.

Hook, Sidney. *Marxism and Beyond*. Totowa, N.J.: Rowman & Littlefield, 1983.

Howe, Irving. "Critic's Return." *New Republic* (Aprl 30, 1990), pp. 43–45.

—— "The Thirties in Retrospect." In Ralph Bogardus and Fred Hobson, eds., *Literature at the Barricades* pp. 13–28. Montgomery: University of Alabama Press, 1982.

—— *World of Our Fathers: The Journey of Eastern European Jews To America and the Life They Found*. New York: Harcourt, 1976.

Howe, Irving and Lewis Coser. *The American Communist Party 1919–57*. Boston: Beacon, 1957.

Hughes, Robert. *Nothing If not Critical: Selected Essays on Art and Artists*. New York: Knopf, 1990.

Hutcheon, Linda. *A Poetics of Postmodernism: History Theory Fiction*. London: Routledge, 1988.

Iserman, Maurice. *If I Had a Hammer: The Death of the Old Left and the Birth of the New*. New York: Basic, 1987.

Jacoby, Russell. *The Last Intellectuals: American Culture in the Age of Academia*. New York: Basic, 1987.

James, Henry. *The American Scene*. 1907. Ed. Leon Edel. Bloomington: Indiana University Press, 1968.

Jameson, Frederic. *Introduction*. In Roberto Retamar, *Caliban and*

*Other Essays*, pp. vii–xii. Tr. Edward Baker. Minneapolis: University of Minnesota Press, 1989.

—— *The Political Unconscious: Narrative as a Socially Symbolic Act.* Ithaca: Cornell University Press, 1981.

Jay, Martin. "Force Fields." *Salmagundi* (Winter-Spring 1990), 85–86:27–32.

Kauffmann, Stanley. "On Films." *New Republic* (September 12, 1983), pp. 24–25.

Kazin, Alfred. *On Native Grounds.* New York: Reynal & Hitchcock, 1942.

—— *Starting Out in the Thirties.* Boston: Atlantic Monthly and Little, Brown, 1965.

Kempton, Murray. *Part of Our Time: Some Ruins and Monuments of the Thirties.* New York: Simon & Schuster, 1955.

Kermode, Frank. *History and Value.* New York: Oxford University Press, 1988.

—— *The Sense of an Ending.* 1967. New York: Oxford University Press, 1968.

Klehr, Harvey. *The Heyday of American Communism: The Depression Years.* New York: Basic, 1984.

Klein, Marcus. *Foreigners: The Making of American Literature 1900–40.* Chicago: University of Chicago Press, 1981.

—— "The Roots of Radicals: Experience in the Thirties." In David Madden, ed., *Proletarian Writers in the Thirties*, pp. 134–157. Carbondale: Southern Illinois University Press, 1968.

Landis, Joseph. "The Sadness of Philip Roth: An Interim Report." In Sanford Pinsker, ed., *Critical Essays on Philip Roth*, pp. 164–171. New York: Hall, 1981.

Langer, Elinor. *Josephine Herbst: The Story She Could Never Tell.* Boston: Atlantic Monthly and Little, Brown, 1984.

Larsen, Neil. *Modernism and Hegemony: A Materialist Critique of Agency.* Minneapolis: University of Minnesota Press, 1990.

Lasch, Christopher. *The Agony of the American Left.* New York: Vintage, 1969.

—— *The New Radicalism in America.* 1965. New York: Vintage, 1967.

LeClair, Tom and Larry McCaffrey, eds. *Anything Can Happen: Interviews With Contemporary American Novelists.* Carbondale: Southern Illinois University Press, 1983.

Leitch, Vincent. *American Literary Criticism From the 30s to the 80s.* New York: Columbia University Press, 1988.

—— *Deconstructive Criticism: An Advanced Introduction.* New York: Columbia University Press, 1983.

Lentricchia, Frank. *Ariel and the Police.* Madison: University of Wisconsin Press, 1988.

—— *Criticism and Social Change.* Chicago: University of Chicago Press, 1982.

—— "Someone Reading." In Lentricchia and Thomas Mc-Laughlin, eds., *Critical Terms for Literary Study,* pp. 321–338. Chicago: University of Chicago Press, 1989.

Levine, Lawrence. *Highbrow/Lowbrow: The Emergence of Cultural Hierarchy in America.* Cambridge: Harvard University Press, 1988.

Lewis, Sinclair. "The American Fear of Literature." In Seymour Gross and Milton Stern, eds., *Viking Survey of American Literature: The Twentieth Century,* pp. 102–116. New York: Viking, 1975.

Lowenfish, Leon. "The Amerian Testament of a Revolutionary." *Columbia Library Columns* (February 27, 1978), pp. 3–13.

Lukács, Georg. *Realism In Our Times: Literature and the Class Struggle.* Tr. John and Necke Mander. New York: Harper Torchbooks, 1964.

Lynn, Kenneth. "Adams' American Eden." *Washington Post Book World* (June 1, 1980), p. 5.

—— *Airliner to Seattle: Studies in Literature and Historical Writing About America.* Chicago: University of Chicago Press, 1983.

Lyons, Eugene. *The Red Decade: The Stalinist Penetration of America.* Indianapolis: Bobbs-Merrill, 1941.

McConnell, Gary. *Joseph Freeman: A Personal Odyssey From Romance to Revolution.* Ph.D. diss. University of North Carolina, 1985.

Mackaye, Percy. *Caliban By the Yellow Sands.* New York: Doubleday, 1916.

MacLeish, Archibald. *The Irresponsibles.* New York: Duell Sloan, 1940.

Madden, David, ed. *Proletarian Writers of the Thirties.* Carbondale: Southern Illinois University Press, 1968.

Marx, Karl. "From *The Eighteenth of Brumaire of Louis Bonaparte.*" In Eugene Kamenska, ed. and tr., *The Portable Karl Marx,* pp. 287–323. New York: Penguin, 1983.

Marx, Karl and Friedrich Engels. "From *The German Ideology.*" In Eugene Kamenska, ed. and tr., *The Portable Karl Marx,* pp. 162–197. New York: Penguin, 1983.

Menand, Louis. "Don't Think Twice." *New Republic* (October 9, 1989), pp. 18–23.

Miller, Donald. *Lewis Mumford: A Life.* New York: Weidenfeld & Nicolson, 1989.

Mott, Frank Luther. *A History of American Magazines 1850–65.* Cambridge: Harvard University Press, 1938.

Moynihan, Daniel Patrick. "Almost Midnight: Restraint, Mr. Bush." *New York Times* (January 15, 1991), A19.

Mumford, Lewis. *Interpretations and Forecasts: Studies in Literature, History, Biography, Technics, and Contemporary Society.* New York: Harcourt, 1973.

—— *Sketches From Life: the Autobiography of Lewis Mumford—The Early Years.* Boston: Beacon, 1983.

Nadel, Alan. *Invisible Criticism: Ralph Ellison and the American Canon.* Iowa City: University of Iowa Press, 1988.

Nelson, Cary. *Repression and Recovery: Modern American Poetry and the Politics of Cultural Memory.* Madison: University of Wisconsin Press, 1989.

Olster, Stacy. *Reminiscence and Re-Creation in Contemporary American Fiction.* New York: Cambridge University Press, 1989.

Orvell, Miles. *The Real Thing: Imitation and Authenticity in American Culture, 1880–1840.* Chapel Hill: University of North Carolina Press, 1989.

Payne, Kenneth. "Naturalism and the Proletarians: The Case of Mike Gold." *Anglo-American Studies* (April 1983), pp. 21–37.

Pinsker, Sanford. *The Comedy That Hoits: An Essay on the Fiction of Philip Roth.* Columbia: University of Missouri Press, 1975.

Pinsker, Sanford, ed. *Critical Essays on Philip Roth.* New York: Hall, 1981.

Poirier, Richard. *The Renewal of Literature: Emersonian Reflections.* New Haven: Yale University Press, 1988.

Pyros, John. *Michael Gold: Dean of American Proletarian Writers.* New York: Dramatikon, 1979.

Rahv, Philip. *Literature and the Sixth Sense.* Boston: Houghton Mifflin, 1969.

Ramazani, R. J. "Yeats: Tragic Joy and the Sublime." *PMLA* (1989), 104(2):163–77.

Rampersad, Arnold. *The Life of Langston Hughes.* Vol. 1. New York: Oxford University Press, 1986.

Retamar, Roberto. *Caliban and Other Essays.* Tr. Edward Baker. Minneapolis: University of Minnesota Press, 1989.

Rideout, Walter. *The Radical Novel in the United States, 1900–54:*

*Some Interrelations of Literature and Society.* Cambridge: Harvard University Press, 1956.

Riis, Jacob. *How the Other Half Lives.* New York: Scribners, 1890.

Robbins, Bruce. "Modernism in History, Modernism in Power." In Robert Kiely, ed., *Modernism Reconsidered: Harvard English Studies,* 1:229–246. Cambridge: Harvard University Press, 1983.

Robinson, Ione. *A Wall to Paint On.* New York: Dutton, 1946.

Roeder, George, Jr. "What Have Modernists Looked At? Experiential Roots of Twentieth-Century American Painting." *American Quarterly* (1987), 39(1): 56–83.

Roth, Henry. *Call It Sleep.* 1934. New York: Avon, 1964.

Roth, Philip. *Goodbye Columbus.* 1959. New York: Bantam, 1963.

Rushdie, Salman. "Is Nothing Sacred?" *Granta* (Spring 1990), 31:97–112.

—— "A Pen Against the Sword in Good Faith." *Newsweek* (February 12, 1990), pp. 52–57.

Ryan, Michael. "Why I Am a Communist." *American Literary History* (1989), 1(1): 143–146.

Said, Edward. *The World, the Text, and the Critic.* Cambridge: Harvard University Press, 1983.

Salzman, Jack. "Not M. Gorky but Still Mike Gold." *The Nation* (July 10, 1972), pp. 22–24.

Scheyer, Ernest. *The Circle of Henry Adams: Art and Artists.* Detroit: Wayne State University Press, 1970.

Schiller, Dan. *Objectivity and the News: The Public and the Rise of Commercial Journalism.* Philadelphia: University of Pennsylvania Press, 1981.

Shields, Art. "Mike Gold, Our Joy and Pride." *Political Affairs* (July 1972), pp. 41–51, 58.

Shloss, Carol. *Invisible Light: Photography and the American Writer.* New York: Oxford University Press, 1987.

Simon, Linda. *Thornton Wilder: A Biography.* New York: Doubleday, 1979.

Simpson, David. "The Return to History." *Critical Inquiry* (Summer 1988), 14(4): 721–746.

Singal, Daniel. "Towards a Definition of American Modernism." *American Quarterly* (1987), 39(1):7–26.

Starobin, Joseph. *American Communism in Crisis, 1943–57.* Cambridge: Harvard University Press, 1972.

Steffens, Lincoln. "The Modern Business Building." *Scribners* (July 1897), 22:37–61.

Steiner, George. "Books: B. B." *New Yorker* (September 10, 1990), pp. 113–120.

Stimpson, Catharine R. "President's Column." *MLA Newsletter* (Spring 1990), pp. 2–3.

Stone, Albert, ed. *The American Autobiography: A Collection of Essays.* Englewood Cliffs, N.J.: Prentice Hall, 1981.

Strauss, Harold. "Realism in the Proletarian Novel." *Yale Review* (1938), 28(2): 360–374.

Sussman, Warren. *Culture as History: The Transformation of American Society in the Twentieth Century.* New York: Pantheon, 1984.

Tanenhaus, Sam. "Whittaker Chambers, Man of Letters." *New Criterion* (April 1990), pp. 11–19.

Trachtenberg, Alan. *Reading American Photographs: Images as History: Matthew Brady to Walker Evans.* New York: Farrar Straus/ Hill & Wang, 1989.

Trilling, Lionel. Introduction. In *Collected Stories of Isaac Babel,* pp. 9–37. Tr. W. Morison. 1955. New York: Meridian, 1960.

—— *The Last Decade.* New York: Harcourt, 1979.

—— *Speaking of Literature and Society.* New York: Harcourt, 1980.

Turek, Richard. "Jews Without Money as a Work of Art." *Studies in American Jewish Literature* (Spring 1988), 7:67–79.

Vaughn, Alden. "Caliban in the Third World: Shakespeare's Savage as a Sociopolitical Symbol." *Massachusetts Review* (Summer 1988), 29(2):289–313.

Von Wiegand, Charmion. Interview with Paul Cummings. October–December 1968. Archives of American Art.

Wald, Alan. *The Revolutionary Imagination: The Poetry and Politics of John Wheelwright and Sherry Mangan.* Chapel Hill: University of North Carolina Press, 1983.

Walzer, Michael. *Exodus and Revolution.* New York: Basic, 1985.

Warshow, Robert. *The Immediate Experience: Movies, Comics, Theater, and Other Aspects of Popular Culture.* New York: Doubleday, 1962.

Wechsler, James. *The Age of Suspicion.* New York: Random House, 1953.

West, Cornel. *The American Evasion of Philosophy: A Genealogy of Pragmatism.* Madison: University of Wisconsin Press, 1989.

Wilson, Edmund. *Letters on Literature and Politics, 1912–72.* Ed. Elena Wilson. New York: Farrar Straus & Giroux, 1977.

—— *The Shores of Light.* 1952. New York: Vintage, 1961.

—— *The Thirties: From Notebooks and Diaries of the Period.* Ed. Leon Edel. New York: Farrar Straus & Giroux, 1980.

—— *The Triple Thinkers: Ten Essays on Literature*. New York: Harcourt, 1938.

Williams, Raymond. *Culture and Society: 1780–1950*. London: Chatto & Windus, 1959.

Winters, Yvor. *In Defense of Reason*. Chicago: Swallow, 1943.

Woolf, Michael. "The Haunted House: Jewish-American Autobiography." In A. Lee, ed., *First Person Singular: Studies in American Autobiography*, pp. 198–216. New York: St. Martin's, 1988.

Wright, Richard. *Black Boy*. New York: Harper & Row, 1945.

# Index